Practice Book

Grade 5

Harcourt School Publishers

www.harcourtschool.com

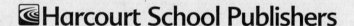

Printed in the United States of America

ISBN 10: 0-15-349879-X
ISBN 13: 978-0-15-349879-4

5 6 7 8 9 10 073 17 16 14 13 12 11 10 09

Contents

RIDE THE EDGE

Rope Burn 1–6

Line Drive 7–11

Chang and the Bamboo Flute 12–17

The Daring Nellie Bly: America's Star Reporter 18–22

Readers' Theater: It Takes Talent! 23–30

The Night of San Juan...31–36

When the Circus Came to Town 37–41

When Washington Crossed the Delaware..42–47

Leonardo's Horse 48–52

Readers' Theater: The Secret Ingredient 53–60

Sailing Home: A Story of a Childhood at Sea...61–66

Ultimate Field Trip 3: Wading into Marine Biology 67–72

Stormalong 73–78

A Drop of Water 79–83

Readers' Theater: How Prairie Became Ocean 84–91

The School Story 92–97

Nothing Ever Happens on 90th Street 98–103

Project Mulberry...104–109

Inventing the Future: A Photobiography of Thomas Alva Edison 110–114

Readers' Theater: The Invention Convention..115–122

Interrupted Journey: Saving Endangered Sea Turtles 123–128

The Power of W.O.W.! 129–134

Any Small Goodness 135–139

Chester Cricket's Pigeon Ride...140–144

Readers' Theater: The Compassion Campaign 145–152

Lewis and Clark 153–158

Klondike Kate 159–163

The Top of the World: Climbing Mount Everest 164–169

The Man Who Went to the Far Side of the Moon...................................170–174

Readers' Theater: Exploring the Gulf Coast 175–182

Index 183–184

Name _____

▶ **Which example is better? Underline the sentence.**

Word	Example 1	Example 2
1. expectations	Julio sees a movie he knows nothing about.	Ian thinks a movie will have a happy ending.
2. fringes	Gary sits by the back door of the restaurant.	Jasmine stands in the center of the room.
3. hesitating	Alma wonders if it is too late at night to call a friend.	Leo is the first one in line to sign up for soccer.
4. humiliation	An actor accidentally trips and falls while he is on stage.	A clown waves to the audience.

▶ **Use what you know about the Vocabulary Words to answer the questions below.**

5. Is someone *sincere* if he really means it when he tells his sister he is proud of her? Explain.

_____

6. Is being *coaxed* into doing something the same as being told to do it? Explain.

_____

_____

School–Home Connection

Discuss the Vocabulary Words and their meanings with your child. Over the next few days, try to use some of the words in conversations with your child.

1

Name _____

▶ Read each section of "Rope Burn." Then fill in the parts of the story map for each section. Include the page numbers on which you found the story elements.

Section 1 | **pages 28–30**   • setting   • characters   • conflict

Setting
- gym (pages 28–29)
- lockers (page 30)

Characters
- Richard (page 30)

Conflict

Section 2 | **pages 32–37**   • setting   • plot events

Plot Events

Section 3 | **pages 38–39**   • setting   • resolution

Resolution

▶ On a separate sheet of paper, write a summary of "Rope Burn." Use the story map to help you.

2

Name _____

▶ Read the story. Circle the sentences that explain the conflict. Underline the sentences that tell the resolution.

> Christy wanted to join her school's cheerleading squad. She knew, though, that several others trying out could do a back handspring, which she could not.
>
> Christy went to Mrs. Michaels, the squad's advisor, for help. Mrs. Michaels explained how to do a back handspring. "Bend your knees. Then jump backward very hard, swinging your arms up. Kick your legs over your head. When your hands touch the ground, push off to return to a standing position." Christy tried the move with Mrs. Michaels spotting her. She was able to do the first parts, but not the landing. She didn't give up, though. Every afternoon she practiced, with her cousin spotting her.
>
> On the day of the tryouts, Christy was well prepared. She performed two perfect back handsprings! Shortly after, she learned that she had been chosen for the squad.

▶ Now fill in the missing information in the graphic organizer.

```
┌─────────────────────────────────────────┐
│                 Conflict                 │
│                                          │
│                                          │
└─────────────────────────────────────────┘
                     ↓
┌─────────────────────────────────────────┐
│               Plot Events                │
│                                          │
│                                          │
│                                          │
└─────────────────────────────────────────┘
                     ↓
┌─────────────────────────────────────────┐
│               Resolution                 │
│                                          │
│                                          │
│                                          │
└─────────────────────────────────────────┘
```

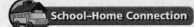

School–Home Connection

Discuss with your child the conflict and resolution in another story your child has read.

Practice Book
© Harcourt • Grade 5

Name _____

▶ Read each story description. Circle the letter of the correct genre.

1. A story about a girl who meets President Abraham Lincoln
   A legend   C folktale
   B historical fiction   D myth

2. A story about a fox and a bear who learn to help each other
   A tall tale   C play
   B realistic fiction   D fable

3. A story about a boy who learns how to tie knots
   A folktale   C realistic fiction
   B legend   D tall tale

▶ Read the following sentences and answer the questions.

> Brady was a fifth-grade student who lived in Colorado Springs with his family. His hobby was taking pictures of birds.

4. Do the sentences describe a character who could appear in a realistic fiction story? Explain your answer.

_____

_____

> There is an island in the Pacific Ocean that is invisible to most people. Ships sail past it and do not know that it is there.

5. Do the sentences describe a place that could be the setting of a historical fiction story? Explain your answer.

_____

_____

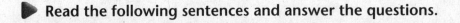

School–Home Connection

Ask your child to describe the characteristics of narrative text. Then discuss stories family members have read or heard that are examples of the different genres.

4

Name _____

▶ **Fold the paper along the dotted line. As each Spelling Word
is read aloud, write it in the blank. Then unfold your paper,
and check your work. Practice spelling the words you missed.**

1. _____

2. _____

3. _____

4. _____

5. _____

6. _____

7. _____

8. _____

9. _____

10. _____

11. _____

12. _____

13. _____

14. _____

15. _____

16. _____

17. _____

18. _____

19. _____

20. _____

Spelling Words

1. bandage
2. chest
3. drift
4. dull
5. dusk
6. stretch
7. flock
8. fond
9. measure
10. cactus
11. scrap
12. shift
13. smash
14. switch
15. swept
16. threat
17. timid
18. plaid
19. trust
20. twist

School–Home Connection

Have your child write the Spelling Words and
underline the letter or letters that stand for
the short vowel sound in each word.

5

Name _____

Complete,
Declarative, and
Interrogative
Sentences

Lesson 1

▶ Circle the interrogative sentences. Underline the declarative sentences.

1. How does Jay like his new school?

2. What does Karen enjoy most about her school?

3. Sara takes piano lessons.

4. Keisha reads magazines about travel.

5. Jay helps Lisa with the math homework.

6. How does Susan prepare for the physical education test?

▶ If the sentence is correct, write *correct*. Rewrite the incorrect sentences correctly.

7. What is the name of the coach.

_____

8. John and Roberto play basketball every Saturday.

_____

9. what does Lisa discover about her new neighborhood?

_____

10. Gale tries out for the volleyball team.

_____

11. Why is Tim waiting to see the teacher.

_____

12. I will look in my desk for the calculator?

_____

School–Home Connection

Work with your child to write a letter about your community. Have your child use two declarative sentences to describe your community and two interrogative sentences to ask about the recipient's community.

Practice Book
© Harcourt • Grade 5

Name _____

▶ **Use what you know about the Vocabulary Words to answer the following questions.**

1. If a person is *exhilarated*, is he completely bored or wildly excited?

   _____

2. If an area is *designated* for swimming, can you swim there or must you stay away?

   _____

3. If someone is a chess *maven*, is she a beginner or an expert?

   _____

4. If a person is *conceited*, does he mostly praise himself or praise others?

   _____

5. If you see a woman with a *smirk* on her face, is she likely to be kind or unkind?

   _____

6. If a girl felt *mortified*, would she more likely dance or hide in a corner?

   _____

7. If a boy *reigned* on a baseball diamond, was he the best player or the worst player?

   _____

School–Home Connection
Discuss the Vocabulary Words with your child.
Work with your child to make up a story using
some of the words.

7

Practice Book
© Harcourt • Grade 5

Name _____

▶ Read each section of "Line Drive." Then fill in the different parts of the story map for each section.

Section 1
pages 58–61

Setting	Characters

Conflict

Section 2
pages 63–67

Plot Events

Section 3
page 67

Resolution

8

Name _____

▶ Read the story. Then fill in the missing information in the story map.

> Van and Lucas were busy wrestling instead of completing the passing drill. Nate really wanted to make the soccer team, but his brothers didn't seem to care.
>
> "Pay attention!" Nate said. "You're making me look bad."
>
> Van and Lucas looked at each other and smiled. Then they jumped on Nate, pushed him to the ground, and started to wrestle again.
>
> "All right. I've had enough," said Coach Holmes. "Van. Lucas. You two belong at wrestling practice. Off to the gym, right now."
>
> Van and Lucas shrugged and headed off to the gym. Nate got up off the ground. "Okay," he said to himself. "Maybe now I can show my soccer skills."

Conflict

Plot Events

1.

2.

3.

Resolution

School–Home Connection

Tell your child a story from your own life in which you overcame a challenge. Talk together about the conflict and resolution in your story.

Practice Book
© Harcourt • Grade 5

Name _____

▶ Fold the paper along the dotted line. As each Spelling Word
is read aloud, write it in the blank. Then unfold your paper,
and check your work. Practice spelling the words you missed.

1. _____
2. _____
3. _____
4. _____
5. _____
6. _____
7. _____
8. _____
9. _____
10. _____
11. _____
12. _____
13. _____
14. _____
15. _____
16. _____
17. _____
18. _____
19. _____
20. _____

Spelling Words

1. needle
2. speech
3. reason
4. crease
5. thief
6. fade
7. obtain
8. faint
9. steep
10. rayon
11. eager
12. shadow
13. kneeling
14. mild
15. coach
16. smoke
17. twice
18. human
19. teenage
20. niece

School–Home Connection

Work with your child to write a sentence for
each Spelling Word. Have your child circle the
vowels in each Spelling Word that spell the
long vowel sound.

Practice Book
© Harcourt • Grade 5

Name _____

▶ **Rewrite the following as imperative sentences.**

1. The batter hits the ball into the outfield.

   _____

2. The outfielder throws the ball to third base.

   _____

3. The hitter bunts the ball.

   _____

4. He tags the runner out.

   _____

5. She steals a base.

   _____

▶ **Label each of the following as an *exclamatory sentence* or an *interjection*. Add a related exclamatory sentence after each interjection.**

6. Oh, no!

   _____

7. The mayor came to the game!

   _____

8. Wow!

   _____

9. We won the championship for the third season in a row!

   _____

10. No way!

    _____

School–Home Connection

Work with your child to write two imperative
and two exclamatory sentences about a sport
other than baseball. Then ask him or her to
add an interjection to one of the sentences.

11

▶ **Which example is better? Underline the sentence.**

Word	Example 1	Example 2
1. pried	Penelope pried open the heavy door.	Penelope pried open an envelope.
2. desperately	Carla searched desperately for her lost car keys.	Carla desperately watched the parade.
3. sneered	Mom kissed me, sneered, and said "Good-night, dear."	The bully sneered and said, "Tough luck!"
4. indignantly	Jeremy indignantly told his boss he was tired of working late.	Jeremy indignantly told his boss he was happy to accept a promotion.
5. urgently	Bea urgently strolled through the park.	Bea urgently called her sister to say that there was an emergency.
6. grudgingly	Sebastian grudgingly agreed to do his chores.	Sebastian grudgingly agreed to eat his favorite dish.

▶ **Use what you know about the Vocabulary Words to answer the questions below.**

7. If someone *desperately* wants to travel to India, does that person have a strong

   desire to visit India? Explain. _____

   _____

8. If you *sneered* at someone, did you act in a friendly, respectful way? Explain.

   _____

   _____

School–Home Connection

Discuss the Vocabulary Words and their
meanings with your child. Over the next few
days, use some of the words in conversations.
Encourage your child to use them, too.

Practice Book
© Harcourt • Grade 5

Name _____

▶ As you read each section of "Chang and the Bamboo Flute," think about what Chang's actions and thoughts tell you about him. After reading each section, answer the questions below.

Section 1 pages 82–83

Character's Traits	Character's Motives
What does Chang do when Mei Mei's father asks him to play the flute?	Why does Chang respond this way? What does this tell you about Chang?

Section 2 pages 84–89

Character's Traits	Character's Motives
What does Chang do when his mother's wok is lost?	Why does Chang do this? What does this tell you about Chang?

Section 3 pages 90–92

Character's Traits	Character's Motives
What does Chang do for the first time when Bo urges him to play the flute?	Why does Chang do this? What does this tell you about Chang?

▶ On a separate sheet of paper, write a summary of "Chang and the Bamboo Flute." Use the graphic organizer to help you.

13

Name _____

▶ **Read the story. Then fill in the missing information in the chart.**

> Brandon loved to play the harmonica, but he didn't feel comfortable playing if other people were listening. So every day after school, he went to his room and played. What he didn't know was that his younger sister, Ginger, hid outside his window and listened to him play. Ginger lay on the grass, closed her eyes, and daydreamed while Brandon played.
>
> One day Ginger heard Brandon become frustrated with his playing. She peeked in the window just in time to see Brandon throw his harmonica into his wastebasket. Ginger thought Brandon would later regret throwing it away. That night while Brandon washed his hands before dinner, she took the harmonica out of the trash and placed it on his dresser.

Ginger's Traits, Thoughts, Words, and Actions	Ginger's Motives
Traits:	
Thoughts:	
Actions:	

School–Home Connection

Discuss with your child the motives of the main character in another story your child has read recently.

14

Practice Book
© Harcourt • Grade 5

▶ **Read the paragraphs below. Use context clues to identify the meanings of the underlined words.**

My brother Alfonzo tried to dissuade our family from going to Aunt Lindy's picnic. He listed several reasons why we shouldn't go. I knew the real reason he didn't want to go. Alfonzo had been learning to play the ukulele, a small guitar with four strings. If we went, my cousins would make him play, and Alfonzo has always been modest. He is the shiest person in our family.

I was glad that our dad decided we would go anyway. We had so much fun! Uncle Enrique took me out in the lake in his rowboat, and we even saw a wading egret. It had white feathers and a long, curved neck. After lunch, my cousins asked Alfonzo for some music, and he played two songs. Everyone was very impressed.

▶ **Circle the letter of the sentence ending that makes the most sense.**

1. If someone tries to dissuade you, that person tries to _____.
   A persuade you not to do something
   B convince you to do something
   C teach you how to do something
   D make you happy

2. A ukulele is a _____.
   A part of a boat
   B type of food
   C lively song
   D musical instrument

3. If someone is bashful, he or she is _____.
   A bold
   B shy
   C a musician
   D very young

4. An egret is a _____.
   A rare type of fish
   B kind of motorboat
   C white bird with a long neck
   D small guitar with four strings

🚌 **School–Home Connection**
Work with your child to use context clues to clarify the meaning of unfamiliar words in a book or magazine article.

Practice Book
© Harcourt • Grade 5

Name _____

▶ Fold the paper along the dotted line. As each Spelling Word is read aloud, write it in the blank. Then unfold your paper and check your work. Practice writing any Spelling Words you missed.

1. _____

2. _____

3. _____

4. _____

5. _____

6. _____

7. _____

8. _____

9. _____

10. _____

11. _____

12. _____

13. _____

14. _____

15. _____

16. _____

17. _____

18. _____

19. _____

20. _____

Spelling Words

1. counter
2. fraud
3. oyster
4. appoint
5. drawn
6. awning
7. laundry
8. feud
9. shawl
10. jewel
11. royalty
12. powder
13. annoying
14. cashew
15. scoop
16. bamboo
17. browse
18. ointment
19. rooster
20. rescue

School–Home Connection

Work with your child to write the Spelling Words in alphabetical order. Then have them write the words in reverse alphabetical order.

16

Practice Book
© Harcourt • Grade 5

Name _____

▶ **Circle the subject and underline the predicate in each sentence.**

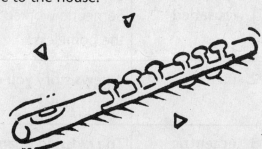

1. The hurricane did not do much damage to the house.

2. The windows were shattered.

3. My friends helped us.

4. I lost my flute in the storm.

5. Angela rushed to the house.

6. My father fixed the roof.

▶ **Write a subject or predicate to complete each sentence. Label the sentence part that you added.**

7. The school _____

8. _____ were broken.

9. Claire _____

10. _____ raised money to help homeless people.

11. The orchestra _____

12. _____ donated clothes and food.

13. Many businesses _____

14. _____ started to clean up the mess.

15. Her parents _____

School–Home Connection

Help your child write three sentences about a community service he or she might participate in. Ask your child to identify the subject and predicate of each sentence.

17

▶ Which example is better? Underline the sentence.

Word	Example 1	Example 2
1. crusaded	Someone worked hard to help the homeless.	Someone drove long distances without stopping.
2. faze	A news story you read upsets you.	A news story you read makes you happy.
3. eccentric	The crossing guard always wears a yellow vest.	The crossing guard always wears purple socks and green shorts.
4. relented	A girl agreed to join the team after first saying no.	A girl would not agree to join the team.
5. impassable	A roadway goes through a mountain pass.	A roadway is blocked by snow.
6. infuriated	A man became very angry about what happened.	A man left the room after the event was over.
7. disheartened	People are hopeful that they will reach a goal.	People have lost hope that they will reach a goal.

▶ Use what you know about the Vocabulary Words to answer the questions below.

8. What is something you would be willing to crusade for? Why?

_____

9. What is something that infuriates you? Why?

_____

School–Home Connection

Have your child write each Vocabulary Word
on a separate slip of paper. Then take turns
choosing a word and using it in a sentence.

18

► As you read "The Daring Nellie Bly: America's Star Reporter," think about what Nellie Bly's actions and thoughts tell you about her. After reading each section, answer the questions below.

Section 1 page 110

Character's Actions and Thoughts

> How does Nellie Bly respond to her editor's doubts?

Character's Motives

> Why does Nellie Bly do this?
>
> What does this tell you about her?

Section 2 pages 111–115

Character's Actions and Thoughts

> What does Nellie Bly do when faced with numerous delays and competition from another reporter?

Character's Motives

> Why does Nellie Bly do this?
>
> What does this tell you about her?

Section 3 pages 116–117

Character's Actions and Thoughts

> What does Nellie Bly do after achieving fame for her success?

Character's Motives

> Why does Nellie Bly do this?
>
> What does this tell you about her?

► On a separate sheet of paper, write a summary of "Nellie Bly: America's Star Reporter." Use the graphic organizer to help you.

Name _____

▶ **Read the paragraphs. Then fill in the missing information in the chart.**

Ethel L. Payne (1911–1991) was a well-known African American journalist. Her career as a reporter began in the 1950s and lasted until the 1980s. An important part of her work focused on the Civil Rights movement.

Ethel Payne is widely remembered for a question she asked at a White House press conference with President Dwight Eisenhower. She asked the President about segregation, or the intentional separation of people of different races. The question shocked President Eisenhower and the other reporters in the room. The President was surprised and seemed upset by the question. The interaction was discussed around the country. It gave special attention to the Civil Rights debate.

Ethel Payne dedicated her career to raising questions about important issues of her time. At one point, while looking back on her career, she said "I fought all of my life to bring about change."

Ethel Payne's Actions, Words, and Traits	Ethel Payne's Motives
Actions:	
Words:	
Traits:	

School–Home Connection

With your child, read a newspaper article about an important person in your community or state. Use the person's words and actions to discuss his or her traits and motives.

20

Practice Book
© Harcourt • Grade 5

Name _____

▶ Fold the paper along the dotted line. As each Spelling Word
is read aloud, write it in the blank. Then unfold your paper
and check your work. Practice writing any Spelling Words
you missed.

1. _____

2. _____

3. _____

4. _____

5. _____

6. _____

7. _____

8. _____

9. _____

10. _____

11. _____

12. _____

13. _____

14. _____

15. _____

16. _____

17. _____

18. _____

19. _____

20. _____

Spelling Words

1. talked
2. hurried
3. smiling
4. dropped
5. clapping
6. stepped
7. worried
8. worrying
9. changing
10. stayed
11. buying
12. dried
13. picnicking
14. scared
15. driving
16. obeyed
17. playing
18. tried
19. carried
20. hurrying

School–Home Connection

Work with your child to write the base word
for each Spelling Word. For example, the base
word for *carried* is *carry*.

21

Practice Book

Name _____

▶ **Add a subject or a predicate to complete each sentence. Label the part you added.**

1. Joseph _____.

2. _____ broke down three blocks from the hotel.

3. The airplane _____.

4. _____ were at the theater.

5. The taxi _____.

▶ **Write a sentence using the simple subject and the simple predicate given.**

6. I, lost

   _____

7. The alarm clock, was

   _____

8. Jessie, telephoned

   _____

9. We, walked

   _____

10. Talisha, saw

    _____

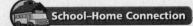
School–Home Connection

Have your child write three sentences using subjects and predicates that you select.

22

Name _____

▶ **Use what you know about the Vocabulary Words to answer the following questions.**

1. If a person is *genial*, is he rude or friendly?

   _____

2. Is *prognostication* telling what is past, or predicting what could happen?

   _____

3. If someone were *stricken* with an illness, would she be very ill or slightly ill?

   _____

4. Would a person behaving *dramatically* show strong feeling or no feeling?

   _____

5. Which might someone need to *restrain*, an angry dog or a sleeping kitten?

   _____

6. If you act in *protest* about something, do you disagree or agree with it?

   _____

7. Which would a person do *feverishly*, fall asleep while reading or work to meet a deadline?

   _____

8. If a person is *overcome* with a feeling, is the feeling strong or mild?

   _____

9. If you saw a movie that was a *flop*, would you be sad or glad that you saw it?

   _____

10. If you saw a *spectacular* movie, would you be sad or glad that you saw it?

   _____

School–Home Connection
Discuss the Vocabulary Words with your child.
Work with your child to make up a story using
some of the words.

23

Practice Book
© Harcourt • Grade 5

▶ Read the story. Circle the paragraph that explains the conflict. Underline the sentences that tell the resolution.

There was one chore Jared hated more than anything—making his bed. However, his mother would not take him to school until it was done.

One morning, Jared and his younger brother, Caleb, were eating breakfast. "I hate making my bed!" said Jared. "I'd do anything to avoid it."

Caleb made a face as he took a bite of his cold, rubbery oatmeal. "Really?" he said. "I like to make beds. I guess that's because I like to have everything neat."

Jared looked at Caleb's cereal. "Are you sure you made that oatmeal right?" Jared asked.

"I don't think so," Caleb said. "I hate making breakfast."

Jared looked thoughtful. "I have an idea!" he said.

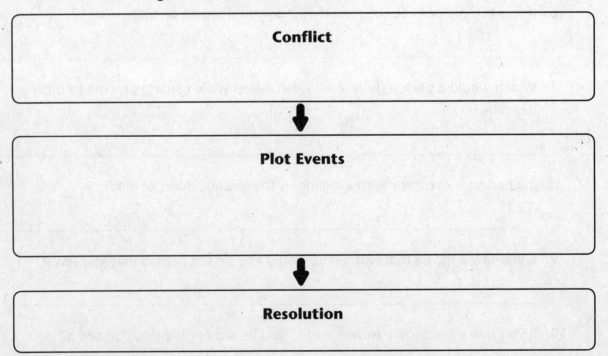

The next day, Jared made two hot breakfasts—one for himself and one for Caleb. At the same time, Caleb made two beds—his and Jared's. As they happily ate together, Jared thought, "I'll never have to make another bed!"

▶ Now fill in the missing information in the chart.

Conflict

⬇

Plot Events

⬇

Resolution

School–Home Connection

With your child, discuss some of the problems of daily life, such as getting ready for school on time or dividing up chores fairly. Discuss the real-life solutions you have come up with.

Practice Book
© Harcourt • Grade 5

Name _____

► Read the story. Then fill in the missing information in the chart.

Dana stood on a tiny platform high up in the treetops. "What am I doing here?" she thought wildly. "I'm afraid of heights!" She touched her "Tree Adventures" badge for good luck. "Come on, Dana, you signed up for this!" she told herself sternly.

Dana looked across the forest clearing. On the other side of it, in another treetop, was the platform she would be jumping to. A wire stretched across the gap, high above the forest floor. Dana knew that she needed to grab the rope that dangled from the wire and swing across the gap to the other platform. She knew that her harness would keep her safe if she lost her grip. Still, her feet felt as if they were nailed to the platform.

Dana took a deep breath. "Ready or not, here I come!" she shouted as loudly as she could. Then she grabbed the rope and leaped into space.

Dana's Thoughts, Words, Actions, and Traits	Dana's Motives
Thoughts:	
Words:	
Actions:	
Traits:	

Practice Book
© Harcourt • Grade 5

▶ **Read each story description. Circle the letter of the answer to tell what kind of narrative text the story is.**

1. a story about a boy who wants to form his own band
   A   a tall tale
   B   historical fiction
   C   realistic fiction
   D   a folktale

2. a story about a cowboy who uses a live rattlesnake for a rope and drains an entire river to water his ranch
   A   realistic fiction
   B   a tall tale
   C   historical fiction
   D   a myth

3. a story about a pioneer girl who crosses America in the 1800s
   A   a folktale
   B   realistic fiction
   C   a fable
   D   historical fiction

▶ **Read the following passage, and then answer the question.**

> Pele is the Hawaiian goddess of the volcano. She uses Pa'oa, her special stick, to dig craters and cause fiery lava to erupt and flow.

4. Does the passage describe a realistic fiction story? Explain your answer.

   _____

   _____

   _____

School–Home Connection

With your child, discuss favorite folktales, legends, and other traditional stories. You might tell your child a folktale he or she does not know.

Practice Book
© Harcourt • Grade 5

▶ Read the passage below. Use context clues to figure out the meanings of the underlined words.

Amelia Earhart was born in 1897. When she was ten years old, she observed her first airplane, at a state fair. At the time, the "thing of rusty wire and wood" did not interest her. Another decade passed. That ten years made a difference. When a stunt plane swooped down at her while she was standing in a clearing, she was suddenly fascinated by flying. Soon afterwards, she took her first flying lesson. This was the beginning of her flying career.

Amelia Earhart set many aviation, or flying, records. She was the first woman to fly solo across the Atlantic Ocean. She set many other solo flying records. She was the first person to fly alone across the country and over the Pacific Ocean. Sadly, she disappeared in 1937 while trying to be the first woman to fly a plane around the world. Amelia Earhart will always be remembered for her courage and her achievements.

▶ Circle the letter of the ending that makes the most sense.

1. When Amelia Earhart observed an airplane at the state fair, she _____.
   A   flew in it
   B   won a prize for building it
   C   noticed things about it
   D   took lessons in it

2. The word aviation has to do with _____.
   A   ancient reptiles
   B   flying
   C   long-distance trucking
   D   women in industry

3. Something that is done solo is done _____.
   A   alone
   B   with a copilot
   C   with a group of people
   D   at a party

School–Home Connection
With your child, create new sentences using each of the underlined words.

27

Name _____

▶ Fold the paper along the dotted line. As each Spelling Word is read aloud, write it in the blank. Then unfold your paper, and check your work. Practice spelling the words you missed.

1. _____

2. _____

3. _____

4. _____

5. _____

6. _____

7. _____

8. _____

9. _____

10. _____

11. _____

12. _____

13. _____

14. _____

15. _____

16. _____

17. _____

18. _____

19. _____

20. _____

Spelling Words

1. stretch
2. cactus
3. measure
4. reason
5. coach
6. kneeling
7. twice
8. rayon
9. appoint
10. scoop
11. drawn
12. feud
13. jewel
14. fraud
15. royalty
16. hurried
17. scared
18. changing
19. buying
20. obeyed

▶ Read this part of a student's rough draft. Then answer the questions below.

> (1) Why does our school have a talent show every year. (2) Our students have some very unusual talents. (3) Javier performs some amazing tricks. (4) Rianna trained her dog to balance a ball on its nose! (5) Make sure to go to the talent show. (6) It is a lot of fun and full of surprises!

1. Which is a correct declarative sentence?
   A Sentence 1
   B Sentence 2
   C Sentence 5
   D Sentence 6

2. Which is an imperative sentence?
   A Sentence 2
   B Sentence 3
   C Sentence 4
   D Sentence 5

3. Which sentence has an incorrect end mark?
   A Sentence 1
   B Sentence 2
   C Sentence 3
   D Sentence 5

4. Which type of sentence is Sentence 1?
   A declarative
   B exclamatory
   C interrogative
   D imperative

5. Which is an exclamatory sentence?
   A Sentence 1
   B Sentence 2
   C Sentence 4
   D Sentence 5

6. Which type of sentence is Sentence 6?
   A declarative
   B exclamatory
   C interrogative
   D imperative

Practice Book
© Harcourt • Grade 5

▶ Read this part of a student's rough draft. Then answer the questions that follow.

(1) I think that Ashley will be a famous violinist some day. (2) Ashley often plays solos in the school concerts. (3) and wins some big competitions. (4) Her teacher has introduced her to some well-known musicians. (5) Ashley practices at least three hours a day. (6) I don't know how she does it!

1. Which is the simple predicate in Sentence 2?
   A Ashley
   B often
   C plays
   D solos

2. Which is the error in Sentence 3?
   A It lacks a subject.
   B It lacks a predicate.
   C It should be interrogative.
   D It should be imperative.

3. Which is the simple subject in Sentence 4?
   A Her
   B teacher
   C introduced
   D musicians

4. Which is the complete predicate in Sentence 4?
   A Her teacher
   B has introduced
   C has introduced her to some well-known musicians
   D well-known musicians

5. Which is the simple predicate in Sentence 5?
   A Ashley
   B practices at least three hours a day
   C at least three hours a day
   D practices

6. Which is the complete subject in Sentence 2?
   A Ashley
   B plays
   C solos
   D concerts

Name _____

▶ **Use what you know about the Vocabulary Words to answer the following questions.**

1. Does a *wistful* person feel happy or sad?

   _____

2. Is a person who feels *grateful* about something you have done likely to thank you or ignore you?

   _____

3. Is a person with a *grim* expression likely to tell you good news or bad news?

   _____

4. Does a *raspy* voice sound rough or smooth?

   _____

5. Would you want to climb a tree if bees *swarmed* near it?

   _____

6. Would you expect *revelers* to dance happily or sit quietly?

   _____

7. What type of fruit do you consider *irresistible*?

   _____

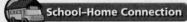
School–Home Connection
Work with your child to invent a story in which you include as many of the Vocabulary Words as you can.

31

Name _____

▶ Read each section of "The Night of San Juan." Complete the sentences in the diagram. Then write the theme of the story.

Section 1 pages 153

Character's Qualities	Character's Actions	Character's Motives
José Manuel's grandma	José Manuel's grandma forbids him from playing on the streets.	José Manuel's grandma thinks the streets are too dangerous.

Section 2 pages 154–159

Character's Qualities	Character's Actions	Character's Motives
Amalia is Evelyn is Aitza is	The sisters come up with a plan to	The sisters want to

Section 3 pages 160–161

Character's Qualities	Character's Actions	Character's Motives
José Manuel's grandma is willing to	José Manuel joins the girls	José Manuel's grandma thinks

Theme:

▶ On a separate sheet of paper, write a summary of "The Night of San Juan." Use the diagram to help you.

Practice Book
© Harcourt • Grade 5

Name _____

▶ Read the story. Then fill in the graphic organizer below.

"That new kid sure looks mean," said Max, nodding in Javier's direction.

"He scares me," said Adra.

I had to admit that I was afraid of Javier as well. He is at least 4 inches taller than anyone else in our class. No one had ever seen him talk or smile.

When lunch was over, we all headed back to class. Adra was showing me her new four-color pen when she bumped into Javier, who was facing the other way in front of his locker. He looked surprised when he turned and found Adra sprawled on the floor.

"Oh, sorry," said Javier. "I guess I was in the way." His voice was soft and kind. He helped Adra to her feet. "Are you okay?" he asked, a look of concern on his face.

Javier's Qualities	Javier's Actions	Javier's Motives

Theme:

School–Home Connection

Discuss with your child the theme in another story your child has read.

33

Practice Book
© Harcourt • Grade 5

Name _____

▶ **Use what you know about genre and about the plot of "The Night of San Juan" to answer the questions below.**

1. What is the genre of "The Night of San Juan"? _____

2. What would you expect the setting, characters, and plot of a story of this genre to be like?

   _____

   _____

3. Does the conflict in"The Night of San Juan" fit the characteristics of realistic fiction? Why or why not?

   _____

   _____

4. Does the resolution in "The Night of San Juan" seem realistic? Why or why not?

   _____

   _____

5. Based on your answers to the questions above, do you think the author has written a good realistic fiction story? Explain your answer.

   _____

   _____

   _____

   _____

 **School–Home Connection**

Ask your child to describe the characteristics of fiction stories. Then talk about the stories you and your child like best, and why you like them.

Name _____

▶ Fold the paper along the dotted line. As each Spelling Word
is read aloud, write it in the blank. Then unfold your paper
and check your work. Practice writing any Spelling Words
you missed.

1. _____

2. _____

3. _____

4. _____

5. _____

6. _____

7. _____

8. _____

9. _____

10. _____

11. _____

12. _____

13. _____

14. _____

15. _____

16. _____

17. _____

18. _____

19. _____

20. _____

Spelling Words

1. drizzle
2. gobble
3. meddle
4. shuffle
5. bundle
6. pickle
7. hobble
8. topple
9. hurtle
10. vehicle
11. struggle
12. wiggle
13. spindle
14. speckle
15. griddle
16. ripple
17. article
18. triple
19. jingle
20. bugle

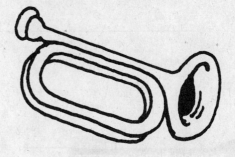

School–Home Connection

Work with your child to sort the Spelling
Words into categories, such as Words with
Double Letters or Words with the Same Vowel
Sound.

Practice Book
© Harcourt • Grade 5

Name _____

▶ **Underline the compound subject in the sentence. Circle the conjunction that joins the subjects.**

1. Jan and Kate make a presentation about our favorite things.

2. Soccer and baseball are the two most popular sports.

3. Chicken, hamburgers, and corn on the cob are my three favorite foods.

4. Milk and juice are two drinks Luis likes.

5. Oatmeal and broccoli are the two foods I like the least.

▶ **Write a sentence with a compound predicate that answers the question. Underline the compound predicate. Circle the conjunction that joins the predicates.**

6. What do you do on a rainy Saturday?

   _____

7. What are three things that you do after school?

   _____

8. What are three things you do with your friends?

   _____

9. What do you do at the beach?

   _____

10. What are two things you do in the morning before you go to school?

   _____

School–Home Connection

Work with your child to write two sentences
that use compound subjects and two sentences
that use compound predicates.

36

Name _____

Robust
Vocabulary
Lesson 7

▶ **Complete the sentences.**

1. An actress might *fret* about an upcoming performance because

_____

2. If your teacher *assured* you that you were ready for the test, you would probably feel

_____

3. She *nudged* the cat curled up in the chair because she

_____

4. A pink dress with big green dots might be described as *outlandish* because

_____

5. A *ruckus* might make a baby cry because

_____

6. A chef *proclaimed* that his food is the best in town because

_____

Practice Book
© Harcourt • Grade 5

Name _____

▶ Read each section of "When the Circus Came to Town." Complete each sentence in the diagram. Then write the theme of the story.

Section 1 pages 180–181

Character's Qualities	Character's Actions	Character's Motives
Ursula	Ursula refuses to go outside and keeps a scarf wrapped around her face.	Ursula does not want

Section 2 page 182

Character's Qualities	Character's Actions	Character's Motives
Ursula is	Ursula agrees to play the harmonica after Ah Sam	Ursula does not want the townspeople to be

Section 3 pages 188–191

Character's Qualities	Character's Actions	Character's Motives
Ursula feels	Ursula stays to play even after	Ursula wants

⬇   ⬇   ⬇

Theme:

▶ On a separate sheet of paper, write a summary for "When the Circus Came to Town." Use the diagram to help you.

▶ **Read the story. Answer the questions that follow.**

Craig's week started with two big tests at school. It ended with a basketball game that went into overtime.

By Friday afternoon, Craig was exhausted. He wanted to spend the evening reading his favorite comic book and catching up on sleep. However, he had promised his grandmother that he would help her carry boxes into her attic.

Craig considered calling his grandmother to cancel. He knew she would be disappointed, but he really wanted to relax. However, the thought of his grandmother's sad voice convinced Craig that he should go.

His grandmother was delighted to see him. She made spaghetti and meatballs, his favorite dinner. When he was leaving, his grandmother gave him a huge hug. Craig was glad he had decided to go.

1. Why does Craig decide to go to his grandmother's house?

_____

_____

2. What does this say about Craig?

_____

_____

3. What is the theme of the story?

_____

_____

School–Home Connection

Discuss with your child the theme in another story that he or she has read.

39

Name _____

▶ Fold the paper along the dotted line. As each Spelling Word
is read aloud, write it in the blank. Then unfold your paper
and check your work. Practice writing any Spelling Words
you missed.

1. _____

2. _____

3. _____

4. _____

5. _____

6. _____

7. _____

8. _____

9. _____

10. _____

11. _____

12. _____

13. _____

14. _____

15. _____

16. _____

17. _____

18. _____

19. _____

20. _____

Spelling Words

1. suppose
2. hurricane
3. ballad
4. bellow
5. success
6. appeal
7. announcer
8. tissue
9. excellent
10. terrific
11. collect
12. slippery
13. common
14. arrange
15. suffer
16. follow
17. kennel
18. squirrel
19. message
20. summary

School–Home Connection

Choose ten words and scramble the letters.
Have your child unscramble the letters and
write the Spelling Words.

40

Name _____

▶ Label the sentence as *simple sentence, simple sentence with
compound subject, simple sentence with compound predicate,
compound sentence, compound sentence with compound subject,*
or *compound sentence with compound predicate.*

1. The clowns make us laugh. _____

2. My favorite performer is not in this show, but I think it will be good anyway.

   _____

3. Noah and I wanted to have our faces painted, but there wasn't enough time before

   the show. _____

4. The clowns and the mimes competed for attention from the audience.

   _____

5. The tigers looked scary, but they obeyed their trainer's commands and behaved very

   well. _____

▶ **Rewrite the sentence correctly. Add a conjunction in the correct place.**

6. Alex had better be on time, I will go into the tent without him!

   _____

7. The balloon artists worked before the show, later, they watched the circus with us.

   _____

   _____

8. We live far from the theater, we arrived on time.

   _____

9. The jugglers struggled, they had too much to handle.

   _____

10. My favorite show is the circus, I go every year!

    _____

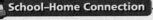

School–Home Connection

Work with your child to write four sentences
about the circus. Include one simple sentence
with a compound subject and one compound
sentence with a compound predicate.

Practice Book
© Harcourt • Grade 5

Name _____

▶ **Use what you know about the Vocabulary Words to answer the following questions.**

1. If you need *persuading* to see a movie, how do you feel about seeing it?

   _____

2. If something is *crucial* for your health, is it very important or not very important?

   _____

3. If soccer players *maneuvered* into position on the field, did they move quickly without thought or skillfully with careful planning?

   _____

4. If a person *encountered* traffic, did the person avoid traffic or come upon traffic?

   _____

5. How might a big storm cause a *crisis*?

   _____

6. If a girl *appealed* to her classmates, did she ask them to do something or tell them to do something?

   _____

7. If a boy showed *perseverance* in learning the piano, was it easy or hard for him?

   _____

8. If a singer thought it was her *destiny* to become famous, did she expect to become famous or hope to become famous?

   _____

School–Home Connection

Discuss the Vocabulary Words with your child.
Work with your child to use at least three of
the words in an oral story.

Practice Book
© Harcourt • Grade 5

▶ As you read each section of "When Washington Crossed the Delaware," fill in the sequence chart below.

Section 1 pages 206–209

```
┌─────────────────────────────────────────────────┐
│                  First Event                      │
│                                                   │
│                                                   │
│                                                   │
│                                                   │
└─────────────────────────────────────────────────┘
```

⬇

Section 2 pages 210–213

```
┌─────────────────────────────────────────────────┐
│                  Next Event                       │
│                                                   │
│                                                   │
│                                                   │
│                                                   │
│                                                   │
│                                                   │
└─────────────────────────────────────────────────┘
```

⬇

Section 3 pages 214–216

```
┌─────────────────────────────────────────────────┐
│                  Next Event                       │
│                                                   │
│                                                   │
│                                                   │
│                                                   │
│                                                   │
└─────────────────────────────────────────────────┘
```

⬇

Section 4 page 217

```
┌─────────────────────────────────────────────────┐
│                  Last Event                       │
│                                                   │
│                                                   │
│                                                   │
│                                                   │
└─────────────────────────────────────────────────┘
```

Practice Book
© Harcourt • Grade 5

Name _____

▶ **Read the paragraph. Then fill in the graphic organizer to show the order of events.**

On the evening of December 16, 1773, a group of men called the "Sons of Liberty" dressed up as Mohawk Indians. They went to Boston Harbor, where three British ships were docked. The ships belonged to a British trading company, and each one held a large shipment of tea. The disguised men quietly climbed on board each ship and then dumped crates of tea into Boston Harbor—45 tons in all. Once the men completed their mission, they fled, removed their costumes, and disappeared into the night. This event, known as the Boston Tea Party, was one of the earliest actions the colonists took against the British. Three years later, the Revolutionary War would begin.

First Event

↓

Next Event

↓

Next Event

↓

Last Event

School–Home Connection

Reread the paragraph with your child, and discuss the words and phrases that give clues about time or the order in which events occurred.

Name _____

▶ **Reference sources can help you find important information. Read each question below. Then choose from the box the reference source you would use to answer each question.**

> dictionary   encyclopedia   almanac
>   atlas   thesaurus

1. What is the correct pronunciation of the word *regiment*?

   _____

2. Where was Thomas Paine born? _____

3. What is a synonym for *revolution*? _____

4. What states border the Delaware River today? _____

5. What museums are located in Washington, D.C.? _____

▶ **Imagine you are doing research on the city of Philadelphia. Next to each reference source, write an example of one thing you might learn about Philadelphia there.**

6. almanac _____

7. newspaper _____

8. atlas _____

9. encyclopedia _____

10. the Internet _____

School–Home Connection

Talk with your child about other sources of information, such as telephone books. Work together to make a list of telephone numbers for families or offices your family calls often.

Practice Book
© Harcourt • Grade 5

Name _____

▶ Fold the paper along the dotted line. As each Spelling Word is read aloud, write it in the blank. Then unfold your paper and check your work. Practice writing any Spelling Words you missed.

1. _____

2. _____

3. _____

4. _____

5. _____

6. _____

7. _____

8. _____

9. _____

10. _____

11. _____

12. _____

13. _____

14. _____

15. _____

16. _____

17. _____

18. _____

19. _____

20. _____

Spelling Words

1. entire
2. hospital
3. public
4. combine
5. golden
6. chimney
7. pretzel
8. survive
9. absorb
10. turmoil
11. wisdom
12. journey
13. condition
14. whisper
15. identify
16. establish
17. furnace
18. capture
19. marvelous
20. nursery

School–Home Connection

Choose ten Spelling Words. Have your child write each word and a word that means the opposite, for example *whisper* and *shout*.

46

Name _____

▶ **Underline the prepositional phrase. Write on the line the preposition and its object.**

1. They sat under a tree.

   _____

2. They fought the battle in the daylight.

   _____

3. The soldiers were stationed around the enemy.

   _____

4. The general watched the cold, wet soldiers step onto land.

   _____

5. The soldiers rose above the challenges and achieved victory.

   _____

▶ **Rewrite the sentence, adding a preposition to fill in the blank.**

6. They carried guns _____ the river.

   _____

7. They hid _____ the bushes.

   _____

8. The soldiers fought _____ freedom.

   _____

9. Another attack _____ dawn was a surprise.

   _____

10. The soldiers were triumphant _____ the end.

   _____

School–Home Connection

Work with your child to write four sentences about American history that include prepositional phrases.

47

Practice Book
© Harcourt • Grade 5

▶ **Use what you know about the Vocabulary Words to answer the following questions.**

1. Would *scholars* of American history know a little or a lot about the history of this country?

   _____

2. If you *specialized* in playing a sport, would you play many different sports or just one?

   _____

3. Which is a *gesture* of friendship: inviting someone to your house or checking out a book at the library?

   _____

4. If you *envisioned* your friend's face, did you see it clearly, or did you have trouble imagining what your friend looked like?

   _____

5. Does a drawing that is in *proportion* look strange and awkward, or does it look natural and realistic?

   _____

6. If a jar of jam *resisted* your efforts to open it, was the jar easy or difficult to open?

   _____

School–Home Connection

Work with your child to write a story in which you include as many of the Vocabulary Words as you can.

Practice Book
© Harcourt • Grade 5

Name _____

▶ Read each section of "Leonardo's Horse." Fill in the
sequence chart below.

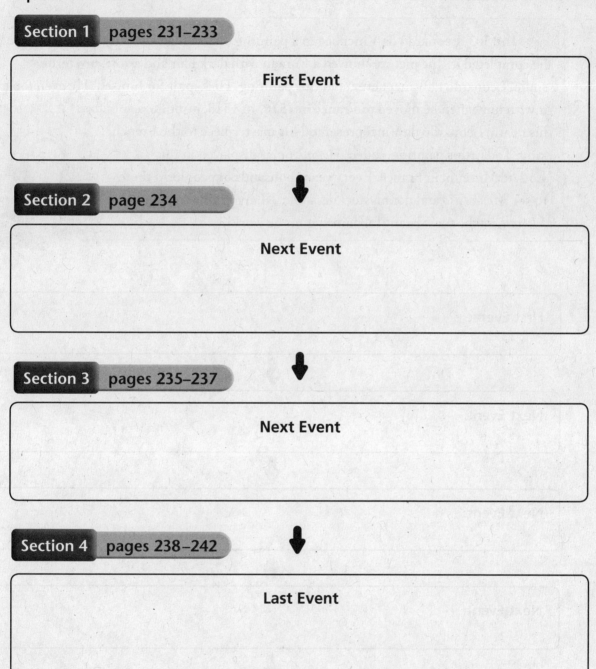

Section 1 pages 231–233

First Event

↓

Section 2 page 234

Next Event

↓

Section 3 pages 235–237

Next Event

↓

Section 4 pages 238–242

Last Event

▶ On a separate sheet of paper, write a summary of "Leonardo's Horse." Use the
sequence chart to help you.

Practice Book
© Harcourt • Grade 5

Name _____

▶ **Read the passage. Think about the way the author organized the information. Then fill in the graphic organizer.**

In 1503, Leonardo da Vinci began a painting of a woman. About three years later, he completed it. The picture showed a woman with dark hair and a soft, mysterious smile. Leonardo da Vinci never sold this painting. He kept it for himself. He even took it with him when he moved to France in 1516. In 1518, just one year before his death, Leonardo da Vinci presented his masterpiece to the French king. Today this painting, called *Mona Lisa*, is displayed in the Louvre Museum in France. Every year, thousands of people go there to see *Mona Lisa* and her mysterious smile. Many people consider *Mona Lisa* the most beautiful painting in the world.

First Event:

⬇

Next Event:

⬇

Next Event:

⬇

Next Event:

⬇

Final Event:

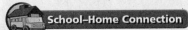

School–Home Connection

Reread the paragraph with your child, and discuss the words and phrases that give clues about time or the order in which events occurred.

50

Practice Book
© Harcourt • Grade 5

Name _____

▶ Fold the paper along the dotted line. As each Spelling Word is read aloud, write it in the blank. Then unfold your paper and check your work. Practice writing any Spelling Words you missed.

1. _____
2. _____
3. _____
4. _____
5. _____
6. _____
7. _____
8. _____
9. _____
10. _____
11. _____
12. _____
13. _____
14. _____
15. _____
16. _____
17. _____
18. _____
19. _____
20. _____

Spelling Words

1. congress
2. English
3. fortress
4. expression
5. conclude
6. complain
7. complex
8. distrust
9. contribute
10. explode
11. umbrella
12. merchandise
13. remembrance
14. concrete
15. goggles
16. portray
17. technique
18. accomplish
19. function
20. membrane

School–Home Connection

Read the Spelling Words aloud. Then have your child sort the words into two categories: words with two syllables and words with three syllables.

51

Name _____

Clauses and
Phrases;
Complex
Sentences

Lesson 9

► Add an *independent clause* or a *dependent clause* as shown in the parentheses to complete the sentence. Punctuate sentences correctly.

1. When the student artist showed his work to the teacher (independent) _____

_____

2. Justin painted standing up (dependent) _____

_____

3. Although the class was nearly over (independent) _____

_____

4. _____ Diane bought some more colored pencils. (dependent)

5. Before Tisha started to paint (independent) _____

► Rewrite the pair of sentences to form a complex sentence. Use the subordinating conjunctions in the parentheses to join the parts of the complex sentence.

6. The students sketched pictures. Then they painted the mural. (before)

_____

7. The students completed the mural. They cleaned up. (after)

_____

8. Jen finished her drawing. She found a place to display it. (when)

_____

9. It was getting dark. The studio's lights were turned on. (because) _____

_____

10. The artist chose bright colors for the painting. The painting showed the countryside on a rainy day. (although) _____

_____

School–Home Connection

Work with your child to write four complex sentences. Ask him or her to circle the subordinating conjunction that joins the parts of each complex sentence.

Practice Book
© Harcourt • Grade 5

▶ **Use what you know about the Vocabulary Words to answer the following questions.**

1. You might see an *eminent* musician play on TV or

   _____

2. Someone who wanted to do an act of *charity* for a community that experienced a terrible hurricane could

   _____

3. A *modest* person would probably never say

   _____

4. A synonym for the word *disgruntled* is

   _____

5. A teacup is an *inadequate* home for aquarium fish because

   _____

6. You would be *aghast* at the way your favorite hat looked if it

   _____

7. If you were cooking, you would be *dismayed* if

   _____

8. You might need to *amend* a piece of writing you have done if

   _____

9. An *absentminded* thing to do with your house key would be to

   _____

10. An example of a very spicy *concoction* would be

   _____

School–Home Connection

With your child, make up oral sentences that use each Vocabulary Word.

Practice Book
© Harcourt • Grade 5

► **Read the story. Then fill in the graphic organizer below.**

As Alden cooked dinner for his family, he thought about how far he had come. He had always been an enthusiastic cook, but he had not always been a good cook.

There was the time when he had mistaken cucumbers for zucchini and baked a really disgusting cucumber casserole. Then there was the time when he had tried to make spaghetti. No one had told him that you have to boil the noodles before you add the sauce. His family had crunched the spaghetti politely, but Alden knew they weren't enjoying it.

Alden smiled to himself, thinking of all the mistakes he had made. Luckily, Alden was a person who never made the same mistake twice. Because of this, and because he had kept on trying, he had finally reached his goal: cooking dinners his family actually enjoyed.

Alden's Qualities	Alden's Motives	Alden's Actions

Theme

Practice Book
© Harcourt • Grade 5

Name _____

▶ Read the passage. Think about the way the author organized the information. Then fill in the graphic organizer.

Lemonade can be a refreshing drink on a hot day. Here's how to make it. First, squeeze the juice from five fresh lemons into a bowl. Then, dissolve one cup of sugar into one cup of warm water. After the sugar is dissolved, pour the mixture into a large pitcher and stir in four cups of cold water. As a variation, you can use carbonated water to make fizzy lemonade. Finally, pour in the fresh lemon juice and stir the liquid well with a spoon. Now your lemonade is ready to enjoy!

First Event

⬇

Next Event

⬇

Next Event

⬇

Last Event

School–Home Connection

Reread the paragraph with your child, and discuss the words and phrases that give clues about time or the order in which events occur.

Name _____

▶ **Use what you know about genre and about the events in "When Washington Crossed the Delaware" to answer the questions below.**

1. What is the genre of "When Washington Crossed the Delaware"?

   _____

2. What is a characteristic of this genre?
   A tells the story of a real person or event   **C** exaggerates people and events
   B has made-up characters and events   **D** uses rhyming words

3. What event does this selection tell about?

   _____

4. How is this selection organized?

   _____

5. Is this an appropriate text structure for this genre?

   _____

   _____

6. What was the author's purpose in writing "When Washington Crossed the Delaware"?

   _____

   _____

7. Based on your answers to the questions above, do you think the author has done a good job? Explain your answer.

   _____

   _____

   _____

   _____

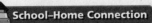
School–Home Connection

Ask your child to describe the characteristics of stories they have read. Then talk about the stories you and your child like best, and why you like them.

Practice Book
© Harcourt • Grade 5

Name _____

▶ Read each question below. Then choose the reference source from the box that could best answer the question. You may choose more than one source.

dictionary	encyclopedia	almanac
atlas	the Internet	thesaurus

1. What is the correct pronunciation of the word *sauté*?

_____

2. Where were tomatoes first grown? _____

3. What is the root of the word *popular*? _____

4. What countries border Italy? _____

5. Where is the nearest cooking school located? _____

▶ Imagine you are doing a report about Italy. Next to each reference source, write an example of one thing you might learn about Italy from that source.

6. almanac _____

7. newspaper _____

8. atlas _____

9. encyclopedia _____

10. the Internet _____

57

Practice Book
© Harcourt • Grade 5

Name _____

▶ Fold the paper along the dotted line. As each Spelling Word
is read aloud, write it in the blank. Then unfold your paper,
and check your work. Practice spelling the words you missed.

1. _____

2. _____

3. _____

4. _____

5. _____

6. _____

7. _____

8. _____

9. _____

10. _____

11. _____

12. _____

13. _____

14. _____

15. _____

16. _____

17. _____

18. _____

19. _____

20. _____

Spelling Words

1. bundle
2. vehicle
3. struggle
4. hurtle
5. triple
6. hurricane
7. golden
8. journey
9. hospital
10. excellent
11. message
12. arrange
13. whisper
14. terrific
15. expression
16. conclude
17. merchandise
18. technique
19. accomplish
20. orchestra

▶ **Read this part of a student's rough draft. Then answer the questions that follow.**

> (1) My friends and I were part of a live audience for a televised cooking show. (2) We watched the preparation of lentil soup, and we saw what happens behind the scenes, too. (3) The chef chopped onion, sliced celery, and diced carrots. (4) He added the vegetables to an oiled pot. (5) He filled the pot with vegetable stock, added the lentils, and brought the mixture to a boil.

1. Which sentence contains a compound subject?
   A Sentence 1
   B Sentence 3
   C Sentence 4
   D Sentence 5

2. Which is a simple sentence with a compound predicate?
   A Sentence 1
   B Sentence 2
   C Sentence 3
   D Sentence 4

3. Which is the subject of Sentence 1?
   A My friends and I
   B audience
   C I
   D cooking show

4. Which is the predicate in Sentence 4?
   A He
   B added the vegetables to an oiled pot
   C the vegetables to an oiled pot
   D an oiled pot

5. Which is the compound predicate in Sentence 5?
   A He filled
   B filled the pot with vegetable stock
   C filled the pot with vegetable stock, added the lentils, and brought the mixture to a boil
   D the mixture to a boil

6. Which of these is a compound sentence?
   A Sentence 1
   B Sentence 2
   C Sentence 3
   D Sentence 4

▶ **Read this part of a student's rough draft. Then answer the questions that follow.**

(1) Our class prepared an international buffet lunch, and it was delicious! (2) Carlos brought tacos, which had meat, beans, corn, and peppers in them. (3) Peter brought pasta because he is Italian. (4) Nicholas brought a Greek pastry called baklava. (5) When I arrived home, I told my mother that I had no room for dinner!

1. Which is NOT a complex sentence?
   A   Sentence 2
   B   Sentence 3
   C   Sentence 4
   D   Sentence 5

2. Which is the dependent clause in Sentence 2?
   A   Carlos brought tacos
   B   meat, beans, corn, and peppers
   C   which had meat, beans, corn, and peppers in them
   D   tacos, which had meat, beans, corn, and peppers

3. Which is the prepositional phrase in Sentence 2?
   A   Carlos
   B   brought tacos
   C   meat, beans, corn, and peppers
   D   in them

4. Which is the prepositional phrase in Sentence 5?
   A   When I arrived home
   B   I told my mother
   C   no room
   D   for dinner

5. Which is the subordinating conjunction in Sentence 5?
   A   When
   B   I
   C   arrived
   D   home

6. Which is the independent clause in Sentence 3?
   A   Peter brought
   B   Peter brought pasta
   C   because he is Italian
   D   because

Name _____

▶ **Which example is better? Underline the best example.**

Word	Example 1	Example 2
1. inflammable	a pile of branches	a stack of bricks
2. dignified	a person who always tells silly jokes	a person who always speaks with a calm voice
3. rowdy	a group of children at a birthday celebration	a group of children in a library
4. seldom	human travel on highways	human travel in space
5. conducted	a person who led a class of students	a person who played an instrument
6. shatter	a drinking glass dropped on the floor	a drinking glass washed with soap
7. broached	a sailboat cutting through a big wave	a sailboat tipped on its side by a big wave

▶ **Answer the questions below.**

8. What is something that *seldom* happens at your school?

_____

_____

9. Would you be more likely to see *rowdy* behavior at a soccer match or at a graduation ceremony?

_____

_____

School–Home Connection

Ask your child to explain to you the meaning of each Vocabulary Word. Work together to use the words in sentences that show their meaning.

61

▶ Read each section of "Sailing Home: A Story of a Childhood at Sea." Then respond to each item to complete the page.

Section 1   pages 278–283

Characters:

Setting:

Section 2   pages 284–287

Conflict:

Plot Events:

Resolution:

▶ Think about the information above. Then, on a separate sheet of paper, write a summary of "Sailing Home: A Story of a Childhood at Sea."

Name _____

▶ Read the paragraph. Then fill in the graphic organizer
below.

The carpenter and the sailmaker were the children's two favorite crew members.
Both were from Scotland and had known the captain for many years. The carpenter
had spent his early years sailing the Atlantic Ocean, unlike the sailmaker, who'd spent
his youth exploring the Pacific. The carpenter made wooden toys for the children,
everything from model sailboats to dollhouses. He also liked to share stories of his
own sea adventures as a young man. The sailmaker made sails for the toy boats, but
spent most of his time teaching the children how to tie knots. Both men always kept
careful watch over the children when they were on deck. Although the two sailors were
different in many ways, they shared a fondness for the children.

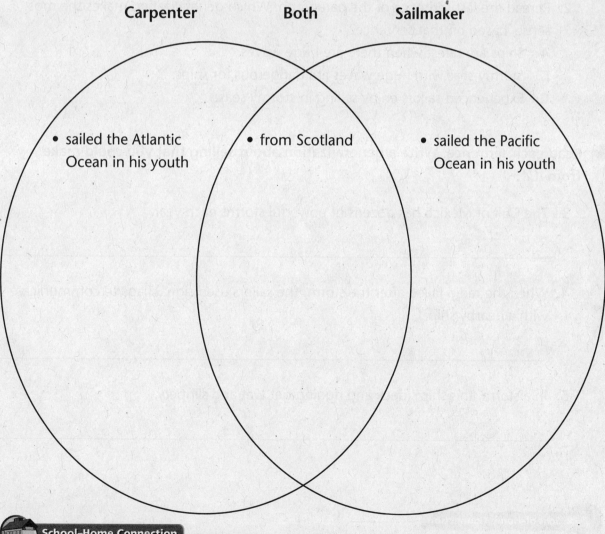

Carpenter   Both   Sailmaker

- sailed the Atlantic Ocean in his youth
- from Scotland
- sailed the Pacific Ocean in his youth

63

▶ Read the paragraph. Then read each question and circle the letter of the correct answer.

> Life aboard a ship is always hard for children. Ships do not have wide-open grassy areas for running and playing. Children have fewer opportunities to make new friends. The options for food on a sailing ship are limited. Worst of all, ships can broach in stormy seas with huge waves.

1. Which of the following statements is a generalization?
   A   Life aboard a ship is always hard for children.
   B   Ships do not have wide-open grassy areas for running and playing.
   C   Children have fewer opportunities to make new friends.

2. Reread the last sentence of the paragraph. Which generalization makes the most sense, based on that sentence?
   A   Ships are safest when there are huge waves.
   B   Stormy seas with huge waves are dangerous for ships.
   C   Experienced sailors enjoy sailing in stormy seas.

▶ Read each sentence. Write a generalization about sailing that you could make from it.

3. The Gulf of Mexico has dozens of powerful storms each year.

   _____

4. When the radio failed after the storm, the sailors used signal flags to communicate with a nearby ship.

   _____

5. In a storm, this ship's deck and rigging get wet and slippery.

   _____

School–Home Connection

Ask your child to make generalizations based on the information in an article or story that he or she has recently read.

64

Practice Book
© Harcourt • Grade 5

Name _____

▶ Fold the paper along the dotted line. As each Spelling Word
is read aloud, write it in the blank. Then unfold your paper
and check your work. Practice writing any Spelling Words
you missed.

1. _____

2. _____

3. _____

4. _____

5. _____

6. _____

7. _____

8. _____

9. _____

10. _____

11. _____

12. _____

13. _____

14. _____

15. _____

16. _____

17. _____

18. _____

19. _____

20. _____

Spelling Words

1. enemy
2. balance
3. basis
4. closet
5. decent
6. define
7. eleven
8. fanatic
9. honest
10. humor
11. minute
12. model
13. protest
14. ocean
15. pretend
16. private
17. radar
18. second
19. slogan
20. editor

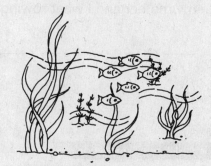

School–Home Connection

Have your child write the Spelling Words,
underlining the words with a short vowel
sound and circling the words with a long vowel
sound.

65

Practice Book
© Harcourt • Grade 5

Name _____

▶ **Underline the common nouns. Circle the proper nouns.**

1. The ship traveled to Alaska.

2. Mr. and Mrs. Pearson were passengers.

3. The crew worked hard to maintain the ship.

4. Spencer and Isabelle played on the deck.

5. Michael went sailing on Lake Garfield.

6. The dishes slid off the tables during the storm.

▶ **Rewrite each sentence with correct capitalization and punctuation. Then underline the proper nouns.**

7. Mr miller greeted the guests on the boat.

_____

8. The boat docked at the marina in monterey, california.

_____

9. We left the port at st augustine, florida, on monday.

_____

10. mrs jenson gazed at the stars.

_____

11. the name of the military ship was the intrepid.

_____

12. my mother and I went rowing on cayuga lake.

_____

School–Home Connection

Work with your child to write four sentences
about a trip. Use both common and proper
nouns in the sentences, including titles of
people and other abbreviations.

66

▶ **Use what you know about the Vocabulary Words to answer the following questions.**

1. How might you *adjust* your behavior if you walked into a room where a baby was sleeping?

   _____

2. What are some animals you would not want to have as *residents* in your attic?

   _____

3. What type of *specimens* might a scientist collect from a beehive?

   _____

4. Would you *recoil* if a rattlesnake was on the path in front of you? Explain.

   _____

5. Would you describe mosquitoes as *pesky*? Explain.

   _____

6. What is one *internal* part of a car? Explain.

   _____

7. What might you expect to find if you went to a beach littered with *debris* from a storm?

   _____

School–Home Connection

Work with your child to look and listen for ways the Vocabulary Words are used in everyday life.

Practice Book
© Harcourt • Grade 5

▶ Read each section of "Ultimate Field Trip 3: Wading into Marine Biology." Fill in the blanks to complete the different parts of the chart.

Section 1   pages 306–309

What makes the tidal zone a difficult place to live? _____

_____

Details that support this idea:

• _____

• _____

Section 2   pages 310–313

What is one of the best ways to learn about the tidal zone? _____

_____

Details about different specimens:

Name of Animal	Unique Characteristic
mussel	uses byssal thread to tie to rock and seaweed
	uses tongue to drill holes in clam shells
sea star	

Section 3   pages 314–319

Why is life in the tidal zone "no vacation for the creatures living there"?

_____

Details that support this idea:

• _____

• _____

▶ On a separate sheet of paper, write a summary of "Ultimate Field Trip 3: Wading into Marine Biology." Use the diagram to help you.

68

Name _____

▶ Read the passage. Think about the way the author
organized the information. Then fill in the graphic organizer.

Squid and octopuses are alike in many ways. They both have soft, boneless bodies and eight arms. Both squid and octopuses are preyed on by some larger ocean animals. When squid and octopuses sense danger, they both have the ability to release a dark fluid, called an ink cloud, to protect themselves. To blend into their surroundings, both creatures have the ability to quickly change the colors and patterns on their bodies.

Because they are so similar, people often think that squid and octopuses are the same. However, a squid has two tentacles in addition to its arms, while an octopus does not. Squid have long bodies and short, compact heads. Octopuses' heads are round and flat. An octopus is able to regrow an arm if it loses one. It is easy to confuse the two animals, but knowing the differences can help you distinguish between them.

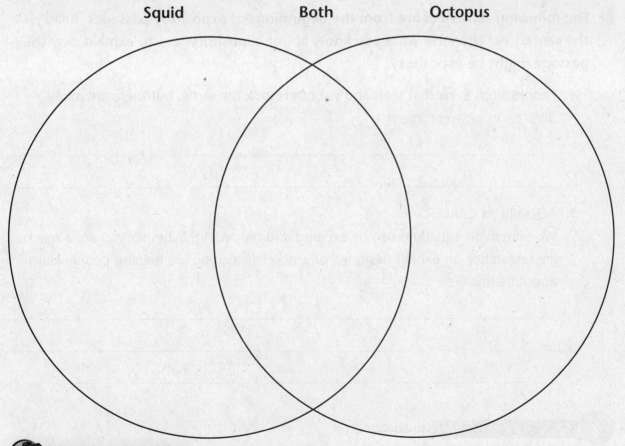

| Squid | Both | Octopus |

School–Home Connection

Discuss with your child the comparisons and
contrasts in a news article he or she has read.

Practice Book
© Harcourt • Grade 5

Name _____

▶ **Read each question. Then circle the letter of the best answer.**

1. Which of the following might be the purpose of an expository text?
   A to entertain people with a story about a talking seagull
   B to give information about an unusual ecosystem
   C to describe a make-believe underwater robot
   D to tell the story of a girl who is scared of the ocean

2. Which of the following is most likely to be an expository text?
   A text that tells a legend
   B text that rhymes
   C text that has stage directions
   D text that explains a process

3. Which of the following features would you NOT find in an expository text?
   A a chart that records the temperatures of the Adriatic Sea
   B photographs of lighthouses with captions telling when they were built
   C dialogue between a sea star and a sea urchin
   D a diagram illustrating the tide cycles

▶ **The following sentences are from the beginnings of expository passages. Read the sentences. Then use what you know about expository text to explain why the passage might be expository.**

4. People often think that seals and sea otters look the same, but there are many differences between them.

   _____

   _____

5. AQUARIUM CAREERS
   Working in an aquarium can be exciting and rewarding. Whether you are a marine life researcher, an exhibit designer, or a ticket seller, you are helping people learn about marine life.

   _____

   _____

   _____

School–Home Connection

Ask your child to describe the characteristics of expository text. Then work together to find examples of expository text in publications, and identify the purpose of each one.

70

Name _____

▶ Fold the paper along the dotted line. As each Spelling Word is read aloud, write it in the blank. Then unfold your paper and check your work. Practice writing any Spelling Words you missed.

1. _____

2. _____

3. _____

4. _____

5. _____

6. _____

7. _____

8. _____

9. _____

10. _____

11. _____

12. _____

13. _____

14. _____

15. _____

16. _____

17. _____

18. _____

19. _____

20. _____

Spelling Words

1. reenter
2. refried
3. reconsider
4. repaint
5. reform
6. replay
7. retake
8. remake
9. reclaim
10. replant
11. unable
12. uninformed
13. undesirable
14. untold
15. unwise
16. nonconductor
17. nonproductive
18. nonexistent
19. nonflammable
20. nondairy

NONFLAMMABLE
GAS

2

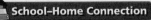

School–Home Connection

Have your child write the prefix and base word for each Spelling Word on separate slips of paper. Use the slips to play a matching game.

71

Practice Book
© Harcourt • Grade 5

▶ **Write the singular form of the plural noun in each sentence.**

1. We wore scarves to go out on deck. _____

2. We caught many fish on the last trip. _____

3. The spies hid in the submarine. _____

4. The sailor made knots along the length of the rope. _____

5. My father wore blue ties when he was in the Navy. _____

6. The crab pot had latches on its side. _____

7. The dolphin navigated by listening for echoes. _____

8. Were the knives kept in a safe place? _____

▶ **Replace all singular common nouns with plurals and rewrite the sentences.**

9. The seagull ate Carl's snack!

_____

10. Be sure to wear rubber boots if you hike through the marsh.

_____

_____

11. The bus traveled daily to the harbor in Massachusetts.

_____

12. He clutched the starfish in his bare hand.

_____

Practice Book
© Harcourt • Grade 5

Name _____

Which example is better? Underline the best example.

Word	Example 1	Example 2
1. bellowing	shouting from a rooftop	whispering into a phone
2. betrayed	a person who was lied to	a person who was congratulated
3. escapades	climbing trees and rafting on rivers in the jungle	skipping to the store and whistling
4. outcast	a person who travels in a group	a person who wanders alone
5. reputation	a person who is known for leading his team to victory	a person who is not known for anything
6. unfathomable	visiting the sun	visiting an island

Answer the questions below.

7. Which might be described as *withered*—dead roses in a vase or blooming roses on a bush? Explain.

_____

_____

8. Why might a basketball player with a broken hand be *yearning* for his or her hand to heal quickly?

_____

_____

School–Home Connection

Discuss the Vocabulary Words with your child.
Have your child write sentences using two
Vocabulary Words in each sentence.

73

▶ Read each section of "Stormalong." Then fill in the story map for each section.

| Section 1 | pages 334–335 | The villagers find a baby alone on a beach. |

Cause

Effect

➡

| Section 2 | pages 336–339 | Stormy moves to Boston when he grows too big for Cape Cod. |

Causes

Effect

↘

↗

| Section 3 | pages 340–347 | Stormy walks to Kansas and becomes a great farmer, but misses the sea and returns to Boston. |

Cause

Effects

↗

↘

▶ Think about the information above. Then, on a separate sheet of paper, write a summary of "Stormalong."

Name _____

▶ **Read the passage. Then fill in the graphic organizers to show the relationships between events.**

The Boccelli family had just begun their voyage to Hawaii when they were caught in a violent storm. Strong winds pushed up big waves that made the boat sway from side to side. As the winds grew even stronger, Alex put away his fishing pole and dropped the anchor. Carlo and Laela lowered the sails. The family gathered below deck to ride out the storm.

Less than an hour later, just as suddenly as it had begun, the storm ended. The sea grew calm and the sky cleared. The sun came out and a light but steady breeze began to blow. So Alex, Laela, and Carlo raised the sails again and resumed their trip to Hawaii.

Cause(s)		Effect(s)

A violent storm with strong winds hits the Boccelli family's sailboat as they begin a voyage. ➡

➡

The storm ends. The sea grows calm.

School–Home Connection

Read aloud to your child a story from a newspaper or a book. Then discuss with your child the causes and effects of the events in the story.

75

Name _____

▶ **Read the passage. Then circle the letter of the best answer to each question.**

> A week earlier, it seemed impossible that we would get a chance to go on *The Wave Rider*. Who would ever let us on the huge sailing ship? I was speechless when we heard the unbelievable news that we had the winning raffle ticket. And now we were being transported to the ship in a small rowboat. As I walked up the ladder, I was filled with happiness. This was an amazing ship—more than 100 feet long, with four stout masts. We spent the rest of the afternoon joyfully wandering the decks. Our time on the ship was absolutely wonderful. My only regret was that we had to disembark before I got to turn the pilot's wheel.

1. Which word does NOT have a prefix?
   A speechless
   B impossible
   C disembark
   D unbelievable

2. What does the word *speechless* mean?
   A the act of speaking
   B speaking again
   C able to speak
   D not able to speak

3. What does the word *wonderful* mean?
   A without wonder
   B full of wonder
   C the act of wondering
   D able to wonder

4. What is the root word of the word *disembark*?
   A dis
   B ember
   C embark
   D bar

School–Home Connection

Ask your child to share with you several word parts—prefixes, roots, and suffixes—that he or she has learned. Together, begin a list of words with these word parts and discuss their meanings. Use a dictionary to confirm the meanings.

76

Name _____

▶ Fold the paper along the dotted line. As each Spelling Word
is read aloud, write it in the blank. Then unfold your paper
and check your work. Practice writing any Spelling Words
you missed.

1. _____

2. _____

3. _____

4. _____

5. _____

6. _____

7. _____

8. _____

9. _____

10. _____

11. _____

12. _____

13. _____

14. _____

15. _____

16. _____

17. _____

18. _____

19. _____

20. _____

Spelling Words

1. development
2. dispensable
3. enjoyable
4. digestible
5. divisible
6. irresistible
7. admissible
8. appointment
9. argument
10. payment
11. amazement
12. priceless
13. judgment
14. resentment
15. embarrassment
16. boundless
17. ageless
18. aimless
19. motionless
20. worthless

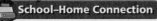
School–Home Connection

Have your child write a story using at least ten
of the Spelling Words. Read the story together.

77

Practice Book
© Harcourt • Grade 5

Name _____

▶ Circle the possessive nouns and label each as *singular* or *plural*.

1. This country's history is very interesting. _____

2. After many days at sea, the settlers' journey ended. _____

3. The people's supplies did not last the entire winter. _____

4. The first colony's population included many children. _____

5. Up until age eight, boys' clothing was the same as girls' clothing. _____

▶ Rewrite the sentences. Replace the underlined words with a possessive noun and the word or words that tell what the noun possesses.

6. The streets of Boston were quiet.

_____

7. Alisha visited the historical sites of the city.

_____

8. I read about the lives of women during colonial times.

_____

9. Rebecca thought the stars and stripes of the flag were a good design.

_____

_____

10. He answered the questions the children had about the *Mayflower* voyage.

_____

_____

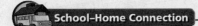
School–Home Connection

List five kinds of animals along with a feature specific to each—for example, *cat* and whiskers. Then ask your child to connect the animals with their features, using possessive nouns.

78

▶ **Underline the sentence that expresses the meaning of each Vocabulary Word.**

Word	Example 1	Example 2
1. elongates	That machine stretches out bread dough.	That old song brings back memories.
2. replenishing	Mom is stirring sugar and milk into her tea.	Mom is refilling the sugar bowl.
3. intricate	Molly helped Mia get a magnet out from under the fridge.	Don put together a model that had lots of small parts.
4. rigid	Dry, uncooked noodles don't bend at all.	The slopes of a roof meet to make an edge on top.
5. accumulate	The fluffy clouds floated by on a breeze.	It snowed so much that it covered the car.
6. elastic	Vera uses a stretchy band to tie her hair back.	Kenny exploded into laughter after Jen told him the story.
7. vanish	My glasses were right here, but now they're gone!	It's taking me forever to paint this wooden cabinet!
8. underlying	Rob told me that petting a lizard makes your hand turn purple.	The basic shape of this flower is a five-sided star.

▶ **Use what you know about the Vocabulary Words to complete each sentence below.**

9. If a pile of laundry was growing larger and larger, you could say that you were

_____ dirty clothes.

10. If you were playing in a small pool and splashed out most of the water, adding

water with a garden hose would be one way of _____ it.

School–Home Connection

Discuss the Vocabulary Words and their meanings with your child. Over the next few days, try to use some of the words in conversation. Encourage your child to use them, too.

▶ Read "A Drop of Water." As you read, answer each question
by filling in the cause-effect chain.

Section 1 **pages 362–363** What causes a water drop to form a sphere as it falls?

Cause	Effect/Cause	Effect
	The surface of the drop shrinks.	

Section 2 **pages 364–365** What causes color to spread throughout a jar of water?

Cause	Effect/Cause	Effect
	Warmed water molecules in the jar move.	

Section 3 **pages 366–369** What causes water vapor to condense into liquid form?

Cause	Effect/Cause	Effect
Water vapor molecules in the air move and bump into things in their path.		

▶ Think about the information above, along with other important ideas you remember
from the selection. Then, on a separate sheet of paper, write a summary of "A Drop
of Water."

Name _____

▶ Read the paragraph below. Think about the way the author organized the information. Then complete the cause-effect diagrams.

The water cycle is the transfer of water from the earth to the atmosphere and back again. When high temperature, low humidity, or wind makes water molecules leave a surface such as the ocean, the water evaporates and enters the atmosphere as water vapor. When enough water vapor is in the air, the air becomes humid. Certain conditions, such as a change in temperature, then make water condense out of the humid air, form clouds, and fall to the ground as rain or snow. Once the water reaches the ground, gravity causes it to make its way as runoff to streams and rivers, which then feed back into the ocean.

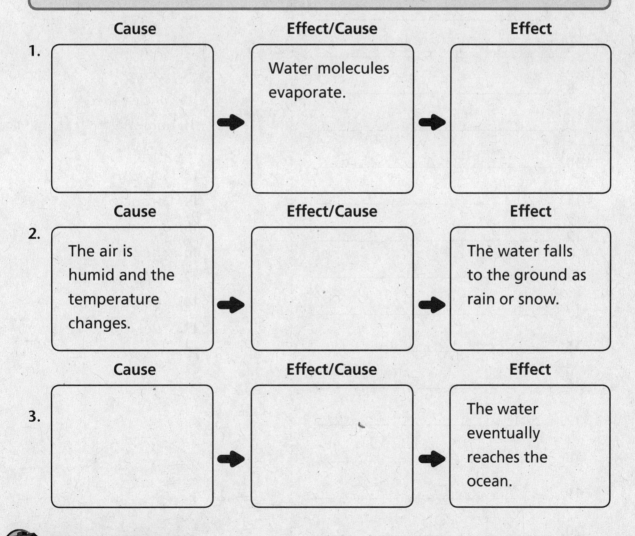

	Cause	Effect/Cause	Effect
1.		Water molecules evaporate.	
2.	The air is humid and the temperature changes.		The water falls to the ground as rain or snow.
3.			The water eventually reaches the ocean.

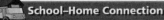

School–Home Connection

Choose a nonfiction magazine or science book to read with your child. Work with your child to identify some cause-and-effect relationships.

81

Practice Book
© Harcourt • Grade 5

Name _____

► Fold the paper along the dotted line. As each Spelling Word
is read aloud, write it in the blank. Then unfold your paper
and check your work. Practice writing any Spelling Words
you missed.

1. _____

2. _____

3. _____

4. _____

5. _____

6. _____

7. _____

8. _____

9. _____

10. _____

11. _____

12. _____

13. _____

14. _____

15. _____

16. _____

17. _____

18. _____

19. _____

20. _____

Spelling Words

1. barrel
2. cannon
3. capitol
4. civil
5. clever
6. discover
7. frozen
8. general
9. hidden
10. inventor
11. mayor
12. pepper
13. polar
14. proper
15. sandal
16. saucer
17. original
18. theater
19. tutor
20. musical

School–Home Connection

Write each of the Spelling Words backwards,
and have your child write the words correctly.

82

Name _____

▶ **Circle the antecedent for each underlined pronoun.**
Write whether the word is *singular* or *plural*.

1. I can't use my bathtub. Water won't go down <u>its</u> drain. _____

2. I telephoned my brothers to ask for help, but <u>they</u> were busy. _____

3. Dinah offered me her tools, but <u>they</u> didn't work. _____

4. The plumber said <u>he</u> can come in the morning. _____

5. Until then, Gina said, I can use the bathtub in <u>her</u> house. _____

6. I asked my landlord if <u>she</u> would pay for the repairs. _____

7. Our lease says that she is responsible. <u>It</u> is in the filing cabinet. _____

▶ **Rewrite the sentences, replacing underlined words with pronouns.**

8. Every winter, my friends call me when <u>my friends</u> know the lake is frozen.

    _____

9. Jason said that <u>Jason</u> would go ice-skating, and I want to go with <u>Jason</u>.

    _____

10. I am meeting Sarah at the lake. <u>Sarah</u> will help me practice skating.

    _____

11. Jenna left <u>Jenna's</u> skates at <u>Jenna's</u> friend's house.

    _____

12. Whenever my mother goes ice-skating, <u>my mother</u> has a good time.

    _____

School–Home Connection

Describe someone or something to your child
using pronouns (*he, she, him, her, they, it,*
etc.). Then ask your child to guess who or what
you are describing. (Example: She likes to play
catch. You give her treats for being good.
Answer: the dog)

83

▶ **Use what you know about the Vocabulary Words to answer the following questions.**

1. Who would *recount* a story, a baby or a mother? Explain.

    _____

2. What could make a planet *uninhabitable*, plenty of water or extreme temperatures?

    _____

3. Which is necessary to *sustain* life in an aquarium, pure water or a goldfish?

    _____

4. What type of landscape do you think is *monotonous*?

    _____

5. Which two words describe an *endeavor—challenging, fluffy, demanding,* or *spacious*?

    _____

6. Where would you like to *dwell*?

    _____

7. Is a *brimming* cup of water filled to the top or halfway full?

    _____

8. What might a pond be *teeming* with?

    _____

9. When might your throat become *parched*?

    _____

10. When might a person be *sorrowful*?

    _____

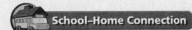

School–Home Connection

With your child, use each Vocabulary Word in
a sentence.

Name _____

► **Read the paragraph. Then complete the graphic
organizer below.**

> Alfred Bulltop Stormalong and Paul Bunyan are both tall tale heroes. These
> characters have many similarities. To begin with, they both came into the world in
> unusual ways. Stormalong was carried onshore by a tidal wave, and Paul Bunyan was
> dropped to Earth by 17 storks. As these giant babies grew up, both of them became
> huge and powerful. They used their strength to do different jobs, though. Stormalong
> became a famous sailor, whereas Paul Bunyan became a great lumberjack. They both
> changed Earth's landscape, too. Stormalong had sailors coat a ship with soap so it
> could slide between the Cliffs of Dover and Calais. The soap made the cliffs white. In
> contrast, Paul Bunyan actually formed the cliffs: he dragged his axe behind him and
> created the Grand Canyon.

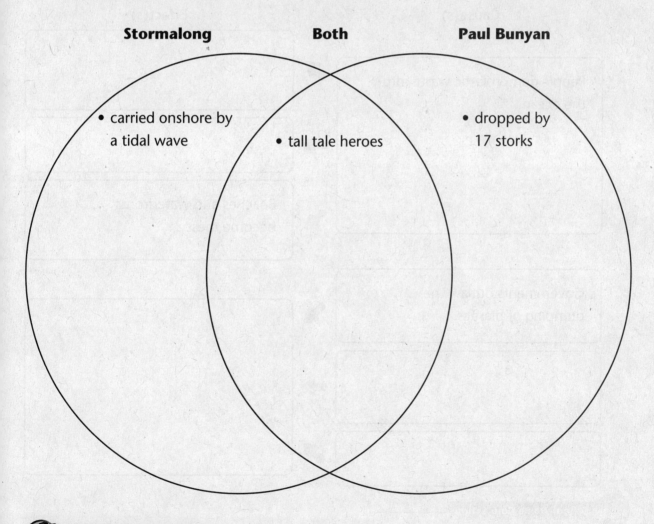

Stormalong   **Both**   **Paul Bunyan**

- carried onshore by
  a tidal wave
                        - tall tale heroes
                                          - dropped by
                                            17 storks

School–Home Connection

Work with your child to compare and contrast
two people you both know.

85

Read the passage. Think about how the author organized
the ideas in the text. Then fill in the graphic organizers to
show the relationships between the causes and the effects.

Plastic products are very convenient. When people dump plastic waste
into the ocean, though, they cause problems. Marine animals become
entangled in everyday items like six-pack rings. Fish mistake plastic bags for
food and eat them, becoming ill or even dying. Some plastic products are carried
to shore by waves, making our beaches and waterfronts messy and unattractive.

Some people are working to improve the situation. Many governments have passed
laws against the dumping of plastics at sea. A number of organizations work to educate
the public. People are recycling and reusing more plastic items, too. People do all these
things so that marine life can become healthier and coastal areas can stay cleaner.

Cause(s)

Effect(s)

People dump plastic waste into
the ocean.

Beaches and waterfronts
become messy.

Governments outlaw the
dumping of plastics.

School–Home Connection

Discuss with your child cause-and-effect
relationships that occur in everyday life. For
example, sleeping through an alarm clock's
ring can cause a person to be late for school.

86

Practice Book
© Harcourt • Grade 5

▶ **Read each question. Then circle the letter of the best answer.**

1. Which of the following might be the purpose of an expository text?

    A   to explain to readers how ocean currents carry nutrients

    B   to tell about an imaginary boat lost at sea in the 1800s

    C   to entertain readers with a humorous story

    D   to retell a traditional tale of bravery at sea

2. Which of the following could NOT be expository text?

    A   text that has main ideas and details

    B   text that is told in sequence

    C   text that is organized by cause and effect

    D   text that has made-up characters, a plot, and a setting

3. Which of the following is more likely to be found in expository text than in other kinds of text?

    A   rhyming lines with descriptive adjectives

    B   an illustration of a misty forest scene

    C   a labeled diagram showing a cross-section of a wave

    D   dialogue between the characters Thunder and Earthquake

▶ **Read the sentences. Then use what you know about expository text to explain why the sentences are from expository passages.**

4. An *upwelling* is a current that brings deep ocean water to the surface. This cold water is usually very rich in nutrients.

    _____

    _____

5. THE OCEAN FLOOR The ocean floor has mountains and valleys, just as land does. The Mariana Trench is a very deep valley on the floor of the Pacific Ocean.

    _____

    _____

School–Home Connection

Ask your child to describe the characteristics of expository text. Then identify examples of expository text in a newspaper or magazine and identify the purpose of each one.

▶ **Read the passage. Then circle the letter of the best answer to each question.**

> Seals are famous for their playfulness. You often see them bobbing in and out of ocean waves. One second they are on top of a wave, and the next second they are gone. They disappear and reappear over and over again. Because they are so likable and fun-loving, seals have been called "aquatic puppies." They even play games, such as chasing and popping the bubbles that scuba divers make!

1. What is the root word in the word *playfulness*?

   A play

   B fulness

   C ful

   D ness

2. Which word does NOT have the same prefix as the word *disappear*?

   A disbelief

   B disembark

   C disrepair

   D dishwasher

3. What does the word *reappear* mean?

   A not appear

   B appear again

   C able to appear

   D not willing to appear

4. What does the word *likable* mean?

   A the act of liking

   B full of liking

   C worthy of being liked

   D not able to be liked

School–Home Connection

With your child, begin a list of words containing prefixes and suffixes that you use in everyday conversation. Add to the list as you use new words.

Practice Book
© Harcourt • Grade 5

Name _____

▶ Fold the paper along the dotted line. As each Spelling
Word is read aloud, write it in the blank. Then unfold
your paper and check your work. Practice writing any
Spelling Words you missed.

1. _____

2. _____

3. _____

4. _____

5. _____

6. _____

7. _____

8. _____

9. _____

10. _____

11. _____

12. _____

13. _____

14. _____

15. _____

16. _____

17. _____

18. _____

19. _____

20. _____

Spelling Words

1. enemy
2. fanatic
3. honest
4. ocean
5. slogan
6. reclaim
7. reconsider
8. uninformed
9. unwise
10. nonexistent
11. digestible
12. enjoyable
13. admissible
14. argument
15. amazement
16. priceless
17. capitol
18. general
19. mayor
20. theater

89

▶ Read this part of a student's rough draft. Then answer the questions that follow.

> (1) I went traveling with my Family over summer vacation. (2) We drove to canada to see the moose. (3) We stopped at niagara Falls and rode a boat called the Maid of the Mist. (4) The spray from the falls soaked my pants, but my brother theo had an extra pair for me. (5) The souvenirs we bought had maple leaf on them, because there is a maple leaf on Canada's flag.

1. Which sentence incorrectly spells a common noun with a capital letter?
   A Sentence 1
   B Sentence 2
   C Sentence 3
   D Sentence 4

2. Which is the correct spelling of the underlined word in Sentence 2?
   A moosies
   B mice
   C mooses
   D correct as is

3. Which word in Sentence 4 should begin with a capital letter?
   A spray
   B pants
   C theo
   D extra

4. Which is an incorrectly capitalized proper noun in Sentence 3?
   A stopped
   B niagara Falls
   C boat
   D Maid of the Mist

5. Which word in Sentence 2 should be written with a capital letter?
   A drove
   B see
   C canada
   D moose

6. Which is the correct plural of the underlined word in Sentence 5?
   A leafs
   B leafes
   C leaves
   D leavs

▶ Read this part of a student's rough draft. Then answer the questions that follow.

> (1) Jason was a hero in Greek mythology, and he sailed a ship called the Argo. (2) The Argos crew members were known as the Argonauts. (3) The Argonauts had many adventures with Jason. (4) One of the missions of the Argonauts was to sail through the Clashing Islands. (5) These two giant cliffs closed in on anything that traveled between _____. (6) Jason's ship was the first one to pass through the cliffs safely.

1. Which is the antecedent for the pronoun in Sentence 1?
   A Jason
   B Greek mythology
   C ship
   D Argo

2. Which is the correct punctuation for the underlined words in Sentence 2?
   A The Argos crew member's
   B The Argos crew members'
   C The Argo's crew members
   D The Argos' crew members

3. Which pronoun can be used to replace the underlined words in Sentence 3?
   A They
   B It
   C She
   D Its

4. Which is the correct possessive phrase for the underlined words in Sentence 4?
   A mission's Argonauts
   B missions' Argonauts
   C Argonaut's missions
   D Argonauts' missions

5. Which pronoun should go in the blank in Sentence 5?
   A they
   B them
   C her
   D he

6. Which word in Sentence 6 is a possessive noun?
   A Jason's
   B ship
   C one
   D cliffs

Name _____

▶ **Complete the sentences.**

1. When the children noticed the tray of fruit in the dining room, they were *tempted*

   to _____

2. A doctor might offer *insights* about _____

3. The *essence* of a good friendship might be _____

   _____

4. One *indication* of an approaching storm might be _____

5. The mayor wished to honor a local hero, so she *proposed* _____

   _____

6. If you tripped on a rock and began to fall, your *instinct* might be to _____

   _____

7. If a traveler was *baffled* about which road to take, he might _____

   _____

🚌 **School–Home Connection**

Ask your child to explain to you the meaning of
each Vocabulary Word. Then have your child use
the word in a sentence to show its meaning.

92

Name _____

▶ Read each section of "The School Story." Then fill in the part of the story map for that section.

Section 1   pages 404–405

Setting	Characters
• Natalie's school	• Natalie

Conflict

Section 2   pages 406–418

Plot Events

Section 3   pages 419–423

Resolution

▶ On a separate sheet of paper, write a summary of "The School Story." Use the completed story map to help you.

▶ Read the story. Use story clues and what you already
know to complete the chart below.

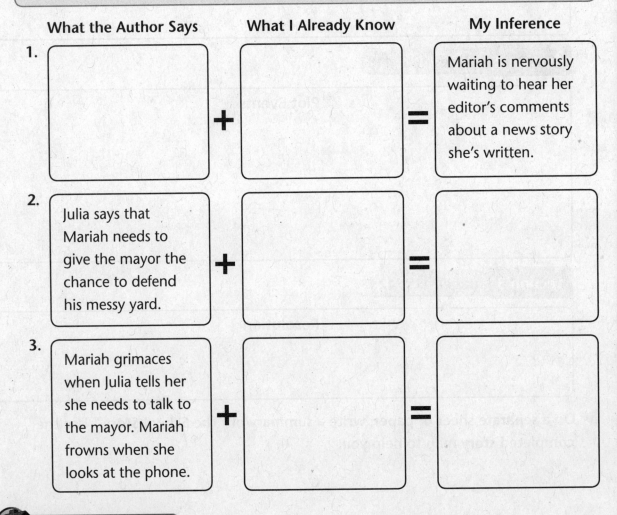

> Mariah paced slowly in front of her editor's office, glancing
> inside. Julia was at her desk, staring intently at the news story on the
> computer screen. Julia didn't look up, so Mariah went back to her desk.
> She played with her hair and then began flipping through her reporter's notebook. Minutes
> went by, but to Mariah it felt like forever. Then Julia was there, standing at her side.
>
> "It's a good story, Mariah. It reads well," said Julia. "But you really need to call the
> mayor's office and get his reaction. I mean, we can't print a story about the messy yard at
> the mayor's house without giving him the chance to defend himself."
>
> Mariah grimaced, but she knew Julia was right. "I'll make the call," she said. As
> Julia headed back down the hallway, Mariah looked at her phone and frowned.

What the Author Says		What I Already Know		My Inference
1.	**+**		**=**	Mariah is nervously waiting to hear her editor's comments about a news story she's written.
2. Julia says that Mariah needs to give the mayor the chance to defend his messy yard.	**+**		**=**	
3. Mariah grimaces when Julia tells her she needs to talk to the mayor. Mariah frowns when she looks at the phone.	**+**		**=**	

School–Home Connection

As you and your child read together or watch
shows on TV, pause periodically to make
inferences about story events. Encourage your
child to explain his or her inferences.

Practice Book
© Harcourt • Grade 5

Name _____

▶ Read the two story summaries below. Then answer each question.

Wind and Sun, an Aesop's fable from ancient Greece

One day Wind and Sun were arguing about who was stronger. They decided to settle the argument by having a contest to see who could make a man on the earth down below remove his coat. Wind went first, blowing strongly. The man wrapped his coat tightly around himself. Then Sun took a turn. It shone brightly and the man felt warm, then hot. Finally, the man removed his coat and sat in the shade.

MESSAGE: Strength is not always defined by who has the greatest force.

Rattlesnake Flies, a folktale from Mexico

Rattlesnake was king of the desert. He was unhappy because he could see his kingdom only from the ground. One day Rattlesnake came upon two crows and asked them if they could help him to fly, so he could see his kingdom from above. The crows found a branch to hold between them. Rattlesnake bit the branch with his sharp fangs. As the crows flew up, they took Rattlesnake with them. Rattlesnake was enjoying the view from high up when Dove landed on the branch next to him. Dove joked that Rattlesnake looked funny flying with a branch in his mouth. Rattlesnake forgot where he was and opened his mouth to strike out at Dove. Immediately, he fell down, down, down, and landed with a thud on the dusty ground. That was the last time Rattlesnake wished to fly.

MESSAGE: Do not try to be something you are not.

---

1. How are the two stories alike? _____

2. How are the two stories different? _____

_____

_____

3. Which of these stories has greater meaning for you? Why? _____

_____

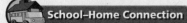
Practice Book
© Harcourt • Grade 5

Name _____

▶ **Fold the paper along the dotted line. As each Spelling Word
is read aloud, write it in the blank. Then unfold your paper
and check your work. Practice writing any Spelling Words
you missed.**

1. _____
2. _____
3. _____
4. _____
5. _____
6. _____
7. _____
8. _____
9. _____
10. _____
11. _____
12. _____
13. _____
14. _____
15. _____
16. _____
17. _____
18. _____
19. _____
20. _____

Spelling Words

1. inactive
2. inaccurate
3. irregular
4. irrelevant
5. ineffective
6. imbalance
7. immature
8. impatient
9. imperfect
10. impossible
11. illegal
12. illiterate
13. illegible
14. inaction
15. independent
16. invalid
17. indefinite
18. injustice
19. irreplaceable
20. impolite

School–Home Connection

Choose ten Spelling Words and have your child
write an antonym, or a word that means the
opposite for each word.

96

Name _____

Subjective and
Objective Case
Pronouns

. . . .
Lesson 16

▶ **Fill in the blank in each sentence with a pronoun.**

1. Mom, Dad, and ____ will visit the home of Laura Ingalls Wilder.

2. The museum director has arranged a special tour for Mom, Dad, and ____.

3. "Dad and ____ will pack the car," I said.

4. We are taking some of Wilder's books with ____.

5. ____ plan to have a week of fun.

▶ **Write a sentence using each pronoun below. Then write whether the pronoun is used in the *subjective* or *objective* case.**

6. we

_____

7. it

_____

8. him

_____

9. you

_____

10. me

_____

School–Home Connection

Work with your child to make a list of six
singular and six plural nouns. Have your child
replace each noun with the correct pronoun
and use the pronoun in a sentence.

97

Name _____

▶ **Which example makes sense? Underline the answer.**

Word	Example 1	Example 2
1. extravagant	an hour-long bath	a five-minute shower
2. unimaginable	a pig that plays in the mud	a pig that plays the piano
3. gourmet	a fancy meal served on fine china	a plain meal served on paper plates
4. throng	two people listening to a radio	a large group of people listening to a concert
5. embarked	began a trip across Alaska	returned from a trip to the library
6. precarious	a glass of water on the edge of a table	a glass of water in the middle of a table
7. hiatus	taking several classes during the summer	resting for three weeks during the summer

▶ **Answer the questions below.**

8. What is something **extravagant** you have seen?

_____

_____

9. Describe a **gourmet** meal you would like to eat.

_____

_____

School–Home Connection

Ask your child to explain to you the meaning of each Vocabulary Word. Then work with him or her to use it in a sentence that shows its meaning.

98

▶ Read each section of "Nothing Ever Happens on 90th Street." Then fill in the parts of the story map for each section. Record new characters as you encounter them.

Setting	Characters

Section 1 page 445

Conflict

Section 2 pages 445–454

Plot Events

Section 3 page 455

Resolution

▶ On a separate sheet of paper, write a summary of "Nothing Ever Happens on 90th Street." Use the story map to help you.

▶ Read the passage. Then complete the chart below. Combine
what the author says with what you know to make inferences.

> It was the opening night of Sal's Soup Shop. Sal stood at the door of his restaurant
> with a stack of menus in this hand. Then he went back into the kitchen. The cooks were
> leaning on the spotless counter and watching a soccer game on television. Three pots of
> hot soup simmered untouched on the stovetop.
>
> People in Sal's neighborhood had complained for years that there
> wasn't a decent neighborhood café. Now, where was everyone? Sal sighed.
>
> One of the cooks came out of the kitchen. His face was shiny
> with sweat. "Sal, it sure is hot tonight! I bet it is still 90 degrees outside."
>
> Sal had an idea. He wrote on a piece of paper, "Tonight's Special—Cool, Fresh
> Salad." He taped the sign on the door and ran to the kitchen to tell the cooks to get ready.

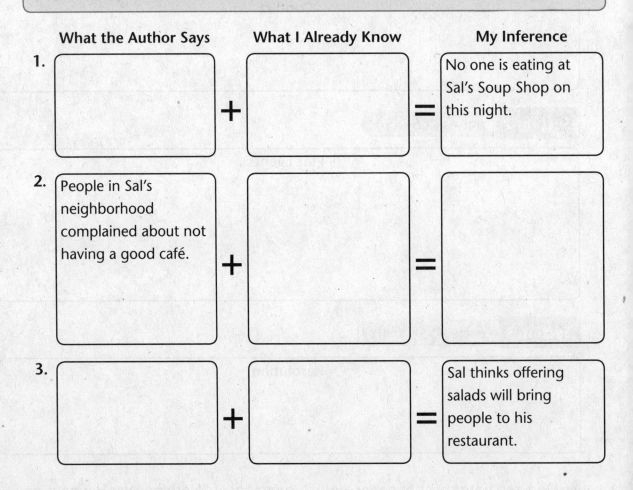

	What the Author Says		What I Already Know		My Inference
1.		+		=	No one is eating at Sal's Soup Shop on this night.
2.	People in Sal's neighborhood complained about not having a good café.	+		=	
3.		+		=	Sal thinks offering salads will bring people to his restaurant.

School–Home Connection

As you read together, encourage your child to
make inferences and explain them.

100

▶ **Read each sentence pair. Then complete the sentence.**

1. The bandit ran from the bank with a bag of money. Another robber was waiting for him in the car.

   A *bandit* is _____.

2. The just supervisor listened carefully to both sides of the argument. She had a reputation for being honest and fair.

   If someone is *just*, he or she is _____.

3. The news reporter was overcome by the exuberance of the fans. He had never seen people so happy and excited before.

   When people show *exuberance*, they are _____.

4. Madeline is wary about trying new foods. Serena, in contrast, is willing to taste just about anything.

   When people are *wary*, they are _____.

5. When I read, I have to concentrate on the story. If something distracts me, I have difficulty paying attention to what I am reading.

   When people *concentrate*, _____.

6. Henry is a professional baseball player, and we like to watch him on television. His brother is an amateur who plays baseball with his friends on weekends.

   When someone is an *amateur* in a particular sport or activity, he or she

   _____.

School–Home Connection

Read a book with your child. Use synonyms and antonyms as context clues to figure out the meanings of new words.

Practice Book
© Harcourt • Grade 5

Name _____

▶ Fold the paper along the dotted line. As each Spelling Word is read aloud, write it in the blank. Then unfold your paper and check your work. Practice writing any Spelling Words you missed.

1. _____

2. _____

3. _____

4. _____

5. _____

6. _____

7. _____

8. _____

9. _____

10. _____

11. _____

12. _____

13. _____

14. _____

15. _____

16. _____

17. _____

18. _____

19. _____

20. _____

Spelling Words

1. accountant
2. applicant
3. attendant
4. defiant
5. mutineer
6. expectant
7. hesitant
8. quadrant
9. resistant
10. servant
11. dependent
12. indulgent
13. insistent
14. urgent
15. auctioneer
16. accompanist
17. artist
18. cellist
19. technician
20. novelist

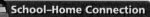
School–Home Connection

Have your child write the Spelling Words. Then have them write the shorter words they find in each word.

102

Name _____

▶ **Circle the correct pronoun in each sentence.**

1. The students will perform a play on (theirs, their) assembly day.

2. Margo has convinced (yourselves, herself) that she should audition for the lead.

3. (Your, Yours) lines are underlined.

4. Please return (my, mine) script after you read it.

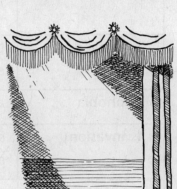

5. The scene she is reading is (her, hers) favorite.

6. The stage needs to have (its, their) boards replaced.

7. Chris, you need to read your lines by (yourself, yours).

8. The students asked (themselves, their) if anyone would come.

9. We need to get (us, ourselves) to the auditorium for the play.

10. On opening night, my father drove (ourselves, himself) to the school.

▶ **Use each pronoun correctly in a sentence.**

11. your _____

12. themselves _____

13. yourself _____

14. its _____

15. hers _____

Practice Book
© Harcourt • Grade 5

Name _____

▶ **Which example is better? Underline the answer.**

Word	Example 1	Example 2
1. compartments	sharp tools for working with wood	small sections to store things in
2. swayed	tall buildings moving in an earthquake	angry bees flying toward a bear near their hive
3. phobia	a love of puppies	a fear of large dogs
4. invasion	six soldiers camping in a forest	1,000 soldiers entering an enemy nation
5. vetoed	accepted an idea for a birthday celebration	rejected an idea for a birthday celebration
6. wispy	a plant with a long, thin stem, skinny branches, and a few leaves	a tree with a short trunk, thick branches, and many leaves

▶ **Answer the questions below.**

7. How could a tray with *compartments* help you keep your school supplies organized?

_____

_____

8. Someone who avoids gardens and anthills might have a *phobia* about _____

_____

School–Home Connection

Discuss the Vocabulary Words and their meanings with your child. Look together for the Vocabulary Words in other stories or magazine articles.

104

Name _____

▶ Read each section of "Project Mulberry." Then fill in the story map for each section.

Section 1 page 470

Characters	Setting

Section 2 pages 471–477

Conflict:

Plot Events:

Section 3 page 478

Resolution:

▶ On a separate sheet of paper, write a summary of "Project Mulberry." Use the story map to help you.

Practice Book
© Harcourt • Grade 5

Name _____

▶ **Read the paragraph below. Look for the main idea and the details that support it.**

For a summer project, Lily and her twin sister, Claire, decided they were ready for a huge challenge: constructing a family tree. Lily began by interviewing their grandparents, aunts, and uncles. Claire visited genealogy websites to collect more information. Both girls looked through old family photo albums, peeling away photographs to check the names and dates on the backs. When they were done with their research, the twins faced a huge pile of notes. Then they began to make a family tree that traced their family history back to the 1800s. They were shocked to find out that there were six sets of twins in their family history!

▶ **Complete the main idea and details web.**

Detail	Detail	Detail

Main Idea
Lily and Claire construct a family tree.

106

▶ **Read the paragraphs below. Then answer the questions.**

A.

Sofia and I just couldn't agree on a topic for our science project. I suggested making a duck skeleton out of cardboard. As usual, that gave Sofia an idea. She wanted to hatch duck eggs and raise the ducklings. I vetoed that idea, since we didn't want to be left with the ducks afterwards. We had to find some way to agree on a topic, or our project would never get started!

B.

Alex sat with her head in her hands. Suddenly she had an idea—what if she and Sofia built a duck skeleton out of cardboard for their science project? Then Sofia said she had a better idea—raising ducklings from eggs. At first Alex thought it it might work, but then she realized that they'd have to find a home for the ducks afterward. "This process isn't working," thought Alex. "We should just make a list of possible topics and pick one."

C.

Alex and Sofia still couldn't agree on a science project. One of them would come up with an idea, such as building a duck skeleton out of cardboard, and that would give the other one another idea, such as hatching live ducklings. Sofia thought Alex's projects were too boring, and Alex thought Sofia's ideas were too difficult. Now they were both starting to think they would never agree.

1. From what point of view is paragraph A written, and how can you tell?

_____

2. From what point of view is paragraph B written, and how can you tell?

_____

3. From what point of view is paragraph C written, and how can you tell?

_____

Practice Book
© Harcourt • Grade 5

Name _____

▶ Fold the paper along the dotted line. As each Spelling Word
is read aloud, write it in the blank. Then unfold your paper
and check your work. Practice writing any Spelling Words
you missed.

1. _____

2. _____

3. _____

4. _____

5. _____

6. _____

7. _____

8. _____

9. _____

10. _____

11. _____

12. _____

13. _____

14. _____

15. _____

16. _____

17. _____

18. _____

19. _____

20. _____

Spelling Words

1. courteous
2. hazardous
3. humorous
4. monstrous
5. porous
6. curious
7. furious
8. glorious
9. delirious
10. fictitious
11. gracious
12. ambitious
13. discourteous
14. dangerous
15. anxious
16. spontaneous
17. religious
18. delicious
19. mountainous
20. ridiculous

School–Home Connection

Have your child write two Spelling Words that
have a common letter so that they criss-cross.
Have them repeat until they write each word.

Practice Book

Name _____

▶ Rewrite each underlined adjective. Then write whether it is an *article* or whether it tells *which one*, *what kind*, or *how many*.

1. The big book fair starts next week at Ring Middle School.

   _____   _____

2. Each student will get one free book with the money raised.

   _____   _____

3. We will donate to the local library all the books that are not sold.

   _____   _____

4. On the third weekend of March, many students will help out.

   _____   _____

5. Few students at the school are not involved.

   _____   _____

▶ Circle the correct form of the adjective.

6. You are the (most funniest, funniest) person I know!

7. Of all my friends, you tell the (better, best) jokes.

8. Between you and your sister, you are the (more clever, most clever) comedian.

9. If you have a day that is (worse, worser) than mine, I'll make you laugh, too!

10. Today is the (greater, greatest) day of my life.

11. We told my sister the (more hilarious, most hilarious) joke of all.

12. I have never seen her (happy, happier) than she was today.

School-Home Connection

Help your child practice using comparative adjectives by comparing things you see around your home. Ask which items are *tallest* or *shortest*, the *more* or *most beautiful*.

109

▶ **Which example is better? Underline the sentence.**

Word	Example 1	Example 2
1. device	The firefighter wore fireproof boots.	The electrician used a special tool to check the wires.
2. industry	1,000 factories worldwide make that product.	This TV is older than that one.
3. feat	"I can't believe you taught yourself Morse code in one afternoon!"	"I wonder how often Morse code is used these days."
4. irrepressible	Ryka made banana bread for the school party.	Paul can't help dancing when he hears lively music.
5. tendency	Bill speaks in a loud voice when he gets angry.	I paid the shopkeeper and she gave me the correct change.
6. prestigious	Dr. Jackson builds model airplanes as a hobby.	Professor Tennen's research earned her an important award.

▶ **Use what you know about the Vocabulary Words to answer each question below.**

7. What is one **industry** you might like to work in someday?

_____

8. What **device** would you like to learn how to use?

_____

Practice Book
© Harcourt • Grade 5

Name _____

▶ Read each section of "Inventing the Future: A
Photobiography of Thomas Alva Edison." Then complete
the main idea and details charts.

pages 496–498   pages 499–500   pages 501–502

1.

| Detail | Detail | Detail |

Main Idea

Thomas Edison was a curious child, which led to his always looking for
solutions to problems.

pages 502–505   page 506   pages 507–509

2.

| Detail | Detail | Detail |

Main Idea

Thomas Edison never stopped doing, and became an important inventor.

▶ On a separate sheet of paper, write a summary of "Inventing the Future: A
Photobiography of Thomas Alva Edison." Use the main idea and details charts and
other major events from each section in your summary.

Practice Book
© Harcourt • Grade 5

Name _____

▶ **Read the paragraph. Then respond to the items below.**

> Have you ever wondered how images find their way onto a television screen? Some TV shows are delivered to homes through over-the-air broadcasting. This method sends electromagnetic waves from a transmitter at a TV station to the antennas in people's homes. Cable TV uses a different method: it delivers signals directly to a TV set through a cable. This direct physical connection usually means that viewers get a better image and better sound. Satellite TV beams television shows all over the world from satellites that orbit the earth. A satellite dish receives the signals. Direct-broadcast satellites can transmit shows over a very wide area, but they cannot deliver local programs.

1. What is the unstated main idea in this paragraph?

   _____

   _____

2. Find and write the most important details that support the main idea.

   A _____

   _____

   B _____

   _____

   C _____

   _____

3. What graphic organizer would you use to record the main idea and details in this paragraph? Draw it in the space below.

School–Home Connection

Reread the paragraph with your child. Help him or her identify details that further explain each method.

112

Name _____

▶ Fold the paper along the dotted line. As each Spelling Word
is read aloud, write it in the blank. Then unfold your paper
and check your work. Practice writing any Spelling Words
you missed.

1. _____

2. _____

3. _____

4. _____

5. _____

6. _____

7. _____

8. _____

9. _____

10. _____

11. _____

12. _____

13. _____

14. _____

15. _____

16. _____

17. _____

18. _____

19. _____

20. _____

Spelling Words

1. steal
2. steel
3. waste
4. waist
5. weak
6. week
7. base
8. bass
9. pain
10. pane
11. flare
12. flair
13. dual
14. duel
15. stationary
16. stationery
17. flower
18. flour
19. sight
20. site

School–Home Connection

Have your child choose five homophone pairs.
Then draw pictures to show their meanings
and label each picture with the correct spelling
of the homophone.

113

Name _____

▶ **Circle the main verb in each sentence. Underline the
helping verb or verbs.**

1. None of the players has missed a single class.

2. Derek will probably get the prize for best science project.

3. Ben is winning the Most Improved certificate this year.

4. Our class has placed first in the science trivia competition.

5. The principal will distribute the awards at the school banquet.

6. We would have liked a larger audience for our play about Thomas Edison.

7. Next month the teacher will have auditions for the next play.

8. She would like that as many students as possible take part.

▶ **Fill in the blank to complete each sentence. Include a verb phrase.**

9. The laboratory repairs _____.

10. The inventor _____ for volunteers.

11. Six workers _____ to help with the new work.

12. There _____ many opportunities to share your ideas.

13. I _____ the team for this project.

14. Kara _____ to make her experiment work.

15. Gloria _____ about inventing something also.

School–Home Connection

Ask your child to write several sentences about
a recent event at school. Ask him or her to
include helping verbs and to underline the
verb phrases.

Name _____

▶ **Which example is better? Underline the answer.**

	Word	Example 1	Example 2
1.	scour	admiring a new ring	searching for a lost ring
2.	appropriate	wearing sandals in the snow	wearing boots in the snow
3.	practical	buying a toolbox full of tools	buying a twelve-foot inflatable poodle
4.	portable	a refrigerator	a cooler
5.	circulate	searching for a seat in a crowded cafeteria	circling the answers on a test
6.	protrude	a triceratops's middle horn	a triceratops's appetite
7.	boisterous	a sleepy old dog	a yapping, squirming puppy
8.	deduction	I figured it out!	I am really confused!
9.	fickle	my friend for life	my new best friend
10.	measly	six noodles for dinner	a plate of spaghetti for dinner

Practice Book
© Harcourt • Grade 5

Name _____

▶ Read the passage. Look at the clues in the passage. Then complete the chart below.

> Byron looked at the pile of letters on his desk and sighed. Each letter said the same thing: *Not interested.* "I guess no one needs an automatic spaghetti-twirling musical fork," Byron thought sadly.
>
> TurboFork was Byron's most brilliant invention. With the push of a button, the end of TurboFork twirled around and around, wrapping spaghetti noodles into a perfect, neat circle. While TurboFork twirled, it played an Italian opera. "Who *wouldn't* want one?" Byron wondered. Yet not one company had agreed to manufacture TurboFork.
>
> Byron heard the familiar clank of the mail slot cover, followed by the sound of letters hitting the floor. "Maybe today," he thought hopefully.

What the Author Says		What I Already Know		My Inference
1. No company has agreed to manufacture TurboFork, Byron's most brilliant invention yet.	+		=	Why is Byron sad?
2.	+	If a company liked an invention, it would probably want to manufacture it.	=	What do companies seem to think about TurboFork?
3. Byron hears the mail being delivered. He thinks, "Maybe today."	+	When you write a lot of letters, you don't get all the responses at once.	=	What is Byron hoping?

School–Home Connection

As you and your child read together or watch shows or movies on TV, pause periodically to make inferences about story events. Encourage your child to explain his or her inferences.

116

Practice Book
© Harcourt • Grade 5

▶ Read the passage below. Look for the main idea and the details that tell more about it.

> A patent is a document that the government gives to an inventor. A patent gives the inventor the rights to his or her invention for a period of time. This means that no one else can copy, make, or sell the invention without the inventor's permission. A patent also gives an inventor official credit for the idea. Patents are important because they protect inventors.
>
> Obtaining a patent takes about a year. Until the patent is issued, an inventor can protect an idea in another way. The inventor can write a description and draw a sketch of the idea, date and sign the document, and seal it in an envelope. Doing this ensures that the idea is protected until a patent is given.

▶ Complete the main idea and details chart.

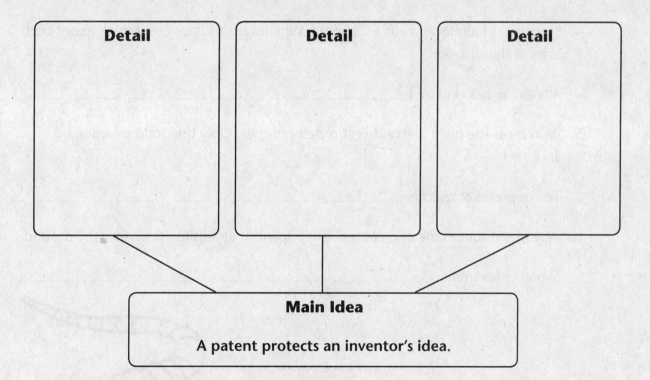

| Detail | Detail | Detail |

Main Idea

A patent protects an inventor's idea.

Name _____

Vocabulary
Strategies:
Synonyms and
Antonyms
• • • • • • • • • •
Lesson 20

▶ **Read each sentence pair. Then complete the sentence below it.**

1. The movie wasn't over, but Sid was <u>dozing</u>. Andy decided to let him keep sleeping.

   Someone who is *dozing* is _____.

2. Anabelle <u>relished</u> the idea of a big, juicy hamburger. At that moment, there was no food she wanted more.

   To *relish* something is to _____.

3. Car alarms <u>perturb</u> my pet parrot. He shrieks unpleasantly when loud sounds disturb him.

   To be *perturbed* is to be _____.

4. Sometimes I am faced with a <u>dilemma</u>. Whenever this happens, I think about both sides of the situation.

   A *dilemma* is a kind of _____.

5. Workers at the plant always <u>reject</u> rotten peaches. Only the good peaches are accepted.

   The opposite of *reject* is _____.

6. Worms are <u>subterranean</u> creatures. They spend their entire lives under the ground.

   Subterranean means _____.

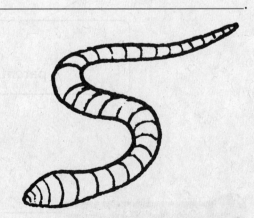

School–Home Connection

Read a book with your child. Use synonyms
and antonyms as context clues to help figure
out the meanings of new words.

Practice Book
© Harcourt • Grade 5

▶ **Read the three paragraphs below. Then answer the questions.**

1.   Jenna hung up the phone and let out a huge cheer. She couldn't believe it—her project had won first prize at the county science fair! A contest judge had just called to tell her the news. Jenna smiled smugly. "Just wait until my know-it-all brother hears," she thought, "and all my classmates, too." Everyone had told her that soybeans were boring. Jenna knew better.

2.   On the day of the science fair, Malik and I entered the auditorium glumly. There was no way our model of the human skeletal system would win. We'd made all 206 bones out of clay. When we had baked the bones in the oven to harden them, some had shrunk. Now the skeleton's legs were shorter than its arms. "We should have built a solar system model," Malik muttered as we placed our ridiculous-looking skeleton on the display table.

3.   Professor DuPont had read all the students' science essays. Now the winner would be announced. Eva shuffled her feet nervously. She was worried that her topic, "Apes of the Ages," was too broad. Next to her, Adley was worried, too. "An Earthworm's Busy Day" had seemed like a good topic, but he'd found so little information that he'd had to keep repeating the same facts. In the front row, Bart was grinning to himself. He was certain that his essay, "X-Ray—Fact and Fiction," would win.

1. What point of view is the first paragraph written in, and how can you tell?

   _____

2. What point of view is the second paragraph written in, and how can you tell?

   _____

   _____

3. What point of view is the third paragraph written in, and how can you tell?

   _____

   _____

School–Home Connection

Ask your child to share with you what he or she has learned about point of view. Then work with your child to rewrite a paragraph from a story in another point of view.

119

Name _____

▶ Fold the paper along the dotted line. As each Spelling Word is read aloud, write it in the blank. Then unfold your paper and check your work. Practice writing any Spelling Words you missed.

1. _____

2. _____

3. _____

4. _____

5. _____

6. _____

7. _____

8. _____

9. _____

10. _____

11. _____

12. _____

13. _____

14. _____

15. _____

16. _____

17. _____

18. _____

19. _____

20. _____

Spelling Words

1. irreplaceable
2. immature
3. indefinite
4. illiterate
5. independent
6. applicant
7. accountant
8. insistent
9. novelist
10. technician
11. cellist
12. porous
13. glorious
14. spontaneous
15. fictitious
16. mountainous
17. weak
18. week
19. dual
20. duel

Practice Book
© Harcourt • Grade 5

Read this part of a student's rough draft. Then answer the questions that follow.

(1) I clean my room each week. (2) Today I ask _____ how I can get the chore done more quickly. (3) I decide to invent a room-cleaning machine! (4) I think that _____ machine will be very successful. (5) I ask my friends if _____ will help me with this plan. (6) We talk among ourselves about how exciting this is!

1. Which pronoun completes Sentence 2?
   A yourselves
   B myself
   C yourself
   D me

2. Which is a subjective case pronoun?
   A I (Sentence 1)
   B the (Sentence 2)
   C my (Sentence 5)
   D ourselves (Sentence 6)

3. Which kind of pronoun is *We* in Sentence 6?
   A subjective
   B objective
   C possessive
   D reflexive

4. Which pronoun completes Sentence 4?
   A him
   B theirs
   C my
   D mine

5. Which pronoun completes Sentence 5?
   A they
   B their
   C themselves
   D your

6. Which kind of pronoun is *ourselves* in Sentence 6?
   A subjective
   B objective
   C possessive
   D reflexive

► Read this part of a student's rough draft. Then answer the questions that follow.

> (1) Peter pulled the sleeping bag tightly around his shoulders. (2) This was the <u>miserable</u> night of Peter's life. (3) Jeremy and Brad _____ shivering just as he was. (4) The wind was slapping the loose tent flap back and forth. (5) Someone <u>should invent</u> a heated sleeping bag, thought Jeremy. (6) Eventually, the three campers fell asleep, and Peter dreamed that he invented the _____ sleeping bag ever!

1. Which helping verb completes Sentence 3?
   A is
   B was
   C were
   D will

2. Which describes the word *loose* in Sentence 4?
   A It is an adjective.
   B It is a pronoun.
   C It is the main verb.
   D It is a helping verb.

3. How should the underlined adjective in Sentence 2 be written?
   A more miserable
   B most miserable
   C less miserable
   D correct as is

4. Which does the adjective *three* in Sentence 6 tell?
   A which one of the campers
   B what kind of campers
   C how many campers
   D the actions of the campers

5. Which adjective completes Sentence 6?
   A good
   B better
   C most good
   D best

6. Which describes the underlined words in Sentence 5?
   A They make up a verb phrase.
   B They are both main verbs.
   C They are both helping verbs.
   D They are adjectives.

▶ **Use what you know about the Vocabulary Words to complete the following sentences.**

1. Someone who has been *basking* in the sun for a few hours might feel _____

   _____.

2. Jet planes are made to be *sleek* because _____

   _____.

3. Somebody who loves animals might believe that a *vital* cause is _____

   _____.

4. Something that would cause *damage* to a forest would be _____

   _____.

5. Someone who enjoys *analyzing* world events might grow up to be a _____

   _____.

6. If you *detect* smoke, you should _____

   _____.

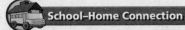

School–Home Connection

Work with your child to find the Vocabulary Words in newspapers or magazines. Discuss how each is used.

123

Name _____

▶ Read each section of "Interrupted Journey." Then fill in the charts.

Section 1 pages 544–547

Detail	Detail	Detail
Turtles can die when they get too cold.		

Main Idea

Section 2 pages 548–549

Detail	Detail	Detail

Main Idea

Stranded turtles are given expert care to help them stay alive.

Section 3 pages 550–553

Detail	Detail	Detail

Main Idea

▶ On a separate sheet of paper, write a summary of "Interrupted Journey." Use the graphic organizers to help you.

124

Practice Book
© Harcourt • Grade 5

▶ Read the paragraph. Use evidence from the paragraph to determine the author's purpose and perspective. Then complete the graphic organizer.

The rhinoceros is one of the largest and most magnificent of all land creatures. There are five species of rhinos— three in Asia and two in Africa. Sadly, all five species face extinction. Although many efforts have been made to save the rhino, the situation remains desperate. Much of the land that has been home to wild rhino populations has been turned into farmland. People also continue to hunt rhinos, even though they are considered endangered. Some African nations have chosen to move wild rhinos to protected areas. All people who love wildlife should immediately do whatever they can to help save the rhino.

Evidence	Evidence	Evidence

Author's Purpose:

Author's Perspective:

School–Home Connection

Read a magazine article with your child, and discuss the author's purpose and perspective.

125

Practice Book
© Harcourt • Grade 5

▶ **Read the passage. Then look at the chart and underline the better example of each persuasive technique.**

The blue whale is the largest animal on Earth. Blue whales are found in all of the world's oceans. Sadly, the blue whale is an endangered animal. Beginning around the 1920s, people started using harpoon guns to hunt blue whales. After about forty years of being hunted, the blue whale was near extinction. The nations of the world then acted to put an end to the hunting. Shockingly, the blue whale is still illegally hunted. Humans are the main cause of the decline in the blue whale population, so only we can save them. It is important that we work to keep the oceans clean, because scientists have shown how dangerous polluted oceans are to the blue whale. Fishermen must obey laws that protect the blue whale. We need to do all we can to save the gentle blue whale, the most majestic of all ocean creatures.

Persuasive Technique	Example
Appeal to Emotions	"Sadly, the blue whale is an endangered animal." "Blue whales are found in all the world's oceans."
Appeal to Logic	"Humans are the main cause of the decline in the blue whale population, so only we can save them." "Shockingly, the blue whale is still illegally hunted.
Appeal to Ethics	"Fishermen must obey laws that protect the blue whale." "Beginning around the 1920s, people started using harpoon guns to hunt blue whales."
Appeal to Authority	"It is important that we work to keep the oceans clean, because scientists have shown how dangerous polluted oceans are to the blue whale." "We need to do all we can to save the gentle blue whale, the most majestic of all ocean creatures."
Word Choice	The blue whale is the largest animal on Earth." "We need to do all we can to save the gentle blue whale, the most majestic of all ocean creatures."

School–Home Connection

Over the next week, work with your child to find examples of persuasive techniques used in magazine and newspaper articles. Listen for uses of persuasive techniques on television news programs.

Name _____

▶ Fold the paper along the dotted line. As each Spelling Word
is read aloud, write it in the blank. Then unfold your paper
and check your work. Practice writing any Spelling Words
you missed.

1. _____

2. _____

3. _____

4. _____

5. _____

6. _____

7. _____

8. _____

9. _____

10. _____

11. _____

12. _____

13. _____

14. _____

15. _____

16. _____

17. _____

18. _____

19. _____

20. _____

Spelling Words

1. incompetent
2. uphold
3. inconsiderate
4. indecisive
5. outrank
6. inhumane
7. inorganic
8. income
9. invertebrate
10. outgoing
11. outpatient
12. outspoken
13. outwit
14. downbeat
15. downgrade
16. downplay
17. downtown
18. uplift
19. upstage
20. uptight

School–Home Connection

Have your child write the Spelling Words two
times and cut the words apart. Turn the words
face down and play a matching game together.

Practice Book
© Harcourt • Grade 5

Name _____

▶ Draw one line under each action verb and two lines under each linking verb. Draw a circle around the direct object if there is one.

1. I wrote e-mails to my friend in New England.

2. She became important to me this year.

3. Dora has a house on the ocean.

4. She sent photographs of sea turtles to me.

5. They looked amazing.

6. I am surprised at their size.

7. Sea turtles lay eggs in the sand.

8. The turtles need a safe beach.

9. Are you certain of that?

10. We became interested in conservation.

11. We felt excited.

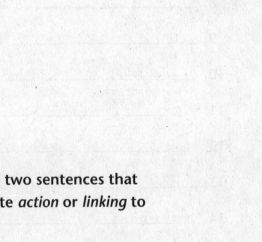

▶ Write two sentences that have action verbs and two sentences that have linking verbs. Underline the verbs and write *action* or *linking* to describe each one.

12. _____

13. _____

14. _____

15. _____

School–Home Connection

Ask your child to write a list of linking verbs. Then ask your child to write a short paragraph about your family, that uses all the verbs on the list.

128

▶ **Which example is better? Underline the answer.**

Word	Example 1	Example 2
1. somberly	telling about a sea turtle that did not survive	announcing the winner of a contest
2. stammers	a professional salesperson	a person speaking in public for the first time
3. monopolize	going to the library and checking out all the books about dogs	going to the library and selecting one book that has information on dogs
4. deflated	a good friend calls to plan a picnic	a good friend cancels a visit
5. enraptured	watching a beautiful sunset	watching traffic go by
6. enterprising	organizing a monthly sidewalk sale	napping on the couch
7. cumbersome	a small backpack with wheels	a heavy backpack with a broken strap

▶ **Complete the items below.**

8. Write a description of something that has *enraptured* you.

_____

9. Describe a time you gave advice to someone who felt *deflated.*

_____

School–Home Connection

Ask your child to explain to you the meaning of each Vocabulary Word and then to use it in a sentence that shows its meaning.

Practice Book
© Harcourt • Grade 5

▶ Read each section of "The Power of W.O.W!" Then fill in the parts of the story map for each section. Include the page numbers where you found the story elements.

Setting	Characters

Section 1 | pages 572–573

Conflict

Section 2 | pages 574–580

Plot Events

Section 3 | page 581

Resolution

▶ On a separate sheet of paper, write a summary of "The Power of W.O.W!" Use the story map to help you.

Practice Book
© Harcourt • Grade 5

Name _____

▶ Read the passage. Look for evidence that can help you figure out the author's purpose and perspective. Use that information to fill in the graphic organizer.

At school, Tyrone noticed that the trash cans were full of two kinds of trash— the kind that can be recycled, like paper and cans, and the kind that can't, like pencil stubs and food scraps. Tyrone's older sister had taught him how important it is for people to recycle. He brought up the subject with his best friend, Marilyn. "Recycling would take so much work!" Marilyn groaned. "We would have to pick through our trash. Eww!"

Tyrone was persistent. He didn't think it would take a lot of work, and he thought it would be worth it. With the help of his sister, he researched the topic on the Internet. Then he approached the school's principal with a plan. The principal praised Tyrone and agreed that the school needed to recycle. Soon everyone, even Marilyn, took pride in separating trash from recyclable materials. They were glad to do their part to protect the environment.

Author's Purpose	Author's Perspective	Evidence

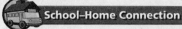
School–Home Connection

Revisit a story you and your child have read recently, and discuss the author's purpose and perspective.

131

Practice Book
© Harcourt • Grade 5

Read the passage. Then complete the chart.

As a volunteer at Oakwood Hospital, Veronica's task is to read aloud to the patients. One day Veronica asked Mr. Levitz what he would like her to read. He sighed. "I really appreciate your visits, but you've already read everything to me—two or three times!"

On her way home, Veronica thought about what Mr. Levitz said. He had a good point. Hearing the same books read over and over is boring. It would be great if she could bring the patients some new books. As she passed the public library, Veronica suddenly stopped in the middle of the sidewalk. She pressed her hand to her forehead and smiled. She had a library card and, for her birthday, she had been given a suitcase on wheels. Veronica formed a simple but brilliant plan.

Textual Evidence	Prior Knowledge	Conclusions

School–Home Connection

Read a story with your child. Use story details and what you know to help your child draw conclusions about story events.

Name _____

▶ Fold the paper along the dotted line. As each Spelling Word
is read aloud, write it in the blank. Then unfold your paper
and check your work. Practice writing any Spelling Words
you missed.

1. _____

2. _____

3. _____

4. _____

5. _____

6. _____

7. _____

8. _____

9. _____

10. _____

11. _____

12. _____

13. _____

14. _____

15. _____

16. _____

17. _____

18. _____

19. _____

20. _____

Spelling Words

1. acceleration
2. accumulation
3. activation
4. alteration
5. authorization
6. calculation
7. cancellation
8. dedication
9. organization
10. demolition
11. repetition
12. mansion
13. pension
14. passion
15. tension
16. champion
17. confusion
18. permission
19. population
20. companion

School–Home Connection

Assign each letter of the alphabet a number
from 1 to 26. Then have your child write the
number code for each Spelling Word.

133

Name _____

▶ **Circle the correct form of the verb in parentheses ( ) to complete each sentence.**

1. The balloons (rise, raise) in the air.

2. The party (celebrate, celebrates) the opening of a new building.

3. Can you (raise, rise) the flag?

4. Our club (present, presents) the money to the director of the hospital.

5. The doctors and hospital staff (sit, set) in the first row.

6. Several kids (lie, lay) on the grass.

7. Other children (play, plays) nearby.

8. The director (thanks, thank) the community for its contribution.

9. I (set, sit) the microphone down on the podium.

10. I (lie, lay) down on the grass, too.

▶ **Rewrite each sentence correctly. Replace the incorrect verbs.**

11. Jeff lays on the sofa and fall asleep.

_____

12. Katie and Jim lie their books on the counter.

_____

13. Paul sits his camera on the shelf.

_____

14. Mia and Kyle watches the sun raising.

_____

15. I cannot rises my sore arm very high.

_____

 School–Home Connection

Ask your child to write a paragraph about flying a kite. Encourage him or her to use the verbs *rise* and *raise*, *lie* and *lay*, and *sit* and *set* in the paragraph.

134

Which example makes sense? Underline it.

Word	Example 1	Example 2
1. gouges	Mike gouges a hole in the ice.	Pete gouges into the phone in a deep voice.
2. desolate	Lani was desolate when she was chosen as a cheerleader.	Parker was desolate when she lost her favorite jacket.
3. bustles	Tran bustles into the hammock for a nap.	Les bustles around his room picking up his belongings.
4. fervor	Sophie talked with fervor about her trip to New York City.	Julia talked with fervor about doing the dishes.
5. immaculate	The car was so immaculate I was afraid I'd sit on something sticky.	After we all pitched in to clean the house, it was immaculate.
6. assuage	To assuage my guilt over a bad grade, I promised to study extra hard.	A good assuage can relax tight muscles.

Answer the questions below.

7. Do you want to laugh or cry when you feel *desolate*?

_____

8. What is an activity that you do with *fervor*?

_____

School–Home Connection

Discuss the Vocabulary Words with your child.
Have your child write sentences, using two
Vocabulary Words in each sentence.

135

▶ Read each section of "Any Small Goodness." Then fill in the parts of the story map for each section. Include the page numbers where you found each story element.

Section 1 pages 595–597

Setting	**Characters**
• the Rodriguez home in Los Angeles (p. 596)	• Arturo (p. 596)

Conflict

Section 2 pages 598–604

Plot Events

Section 3 page 605

Resolution

▶ On a separate sheet of paper, write a summary of "Any Small Goodness." Use the story map to help you.

Name _____

▶ **Read the paragraph.**

> Banjo was lost! Just a few minutes ago, Ned and Banjo had been playing near the creek. Ned threw a ball, and Banjo raced to catch it. Then, just like that, he was gone! Yelling Banjo's name, Ned ran along the creekbed and through the park above it, crunching the red, gold, and purple leaves under his feet. He called Banjo's name again and again, but all he heard was the gurgling of the creek. It was cold—Ned's fingers felt like ice—it was getting dark and Ned trudged home, his heart as heavy as a stone. Even the familiar aroma of stew and the thought of his dad's delicious biscuits couldn't lift his spirits. He took a deep breath and told his parents the horrible news.

▶ **Write touch, sight, taste, smell, or hearing next to each example of imagery from the paragraph.**

Example of Imagery	Sense It Appeals To
red, gold, and purple leaves	
the gurgling of the creek	
fingers felt like ice	
familiar aroma of stew	
dad's delicious biscuits	

▶ **Write an answer to each question.**

- During what season does the story take place? How do you know? _____

_____

_____

- The author says that Ned's heart was "as heavy as a stone." What emotion does

this image suggest? _____

137

▶ Fold the paper along the dotted line. As each Spelling Word
is read aloud, write it in the blank. Then unfold your paper
and check your work. Practice writing any Spelling Words
you missed.

1. _____

2. _____

3. _____

4. _____

5. _____

6. _____

7. _____

8. _____

9. _____

10. _____

11. _____

12. _____

13. _____

14. _____

15. _____

16. _____

17. _____

18. _____

19. _____

20. _____

Spelling Words

1. assign
2. autumn
3. column
4. crumb
5. debris
6. delight
7. design
8. glisten
9. hasten
10. knead
11. knowledge
12. lightning
13. resign
14. rhyme
15. solemn
16. thorough
17. scenery
18. whirl
19. wreath
20. wrestled

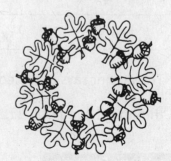

School–Home Connection

Have your child write the Spelling Words and
draw a line through the silent letter in each
word.

138

Name _____

▶ **Rewrite each sentence. Change each verb to its past-tense form.**

1. Jayla will take her kitten to the veterinarian on Saturday.

_____

2. Mr. Vargas smiles at her when she walks past his house.

_____

3. The doctor weighs the cat and checks her for fleas.

_____

4. She announces that the cat's health is excellent.

_____

5. Jayla will give the kitten a treat after the examination.

_____

▶ **Underline the verb in each sentence. Then label each verb as** *present tense*, *past tense*, **or** *future tense*.

6. Molly lives in the city of Los Angeles. _____

7. Molly and Kim planned a day trip to a hiking trail. _____

8. They will ask Milo, too. _____

9. He will arrive after lunch. _____

10. The trail needs better markers. _____

11. The heat made them tired. _____

12. They lose interest in the hiking trail. _____

13. The friends will ride bikes to the beach instead. _____

14. Molly, Kim, and Milo swim in the cool ocean water. _____

School–Home Connection

Ask your child to write four sentences, two about something he or she did last week and two about something he or she plans to do. Ask your child to identify the tense of each verb used.

Practice Book
© Harcourt • Grade 5

▶ **Which example is better? Underline the correct answer.**

Word	Example 1	Example 2
1. excursions	Ken gave two excursions of heroism in the Civil War.	Most kids love going on excursions to the park.
2. giddy	Karen was giddy with delight over winning the trophy.	Bill was giddy from his allergies.
3. precious	Life, liberty, and the pursuit of happiness are precious to Americans.	The children had a precious time prying the lid from the jar.
4. pinnacle	I returned the pinnacle to the library.	The view from the pinnacle of the mountain was breathtaking.
5. gleeful	Monica was gleeful to learn she had won tickets to the concert.	Harry was gleeful when he fell off his bike.
6. panic	I always feel panic when I come to the end of a book.	Tim felt panic when the door slammed shut.
7. turbulent	We had a turbulent day with no new problems.	Flying a kite is more fun when the air is a little turbulent.

▶ **Answer the questions below.**

8. What kind of *excursions* do you enjoy? Why?

_____

9. What kinds of experiences make you *gleeful*?

_____

School–Home Connection

Discuss the Vocabulary Words with your child.
Describe something that is *precious* to you and
something that makes you *gleeful*.

140

Name _____

▶ Read each section of "Chester Cricket's Pigeon Ride." Then fill in the part of the story map for each section. Include the page numbers where you found the story elements.

Setting	Characters
• Times Square (p. 619)	• Chester Cricket (p. 619)
• Central Park (p. 621)	• Lulu Pigeon (p. 619)

Section 1 page 619

Conflict

Section 2 pages 620–629

Plot Events

Section 3 page 629

Resolution

▶ On a separate sheet of paper, write a summary of "Chester Cricket's Pigeon Ride." Use the story map to help you.

Name _____

▶ **Read the passage. Then answer the questions. Use the underlined phrases in your answer.**

Once there was a little black cat who lived in a meadow. Every day, she crept like a shadow through the sea of tall grass, hunting mice and lizards. One day she met a rabbit in the meadow. "What are *you* doing here?" the cat demanded.

"It's a big meadow. Can't we share it?" the rabbit squeaked.

The cat flicked her tail back and forth as she considered the rabbit's suggestion. He sat as still as a post and watched her with eyes as shiny as big black seeds.

Just then the meadow shook as the animals felt the thunder of footsteps pounding toward them. The biggest bull they had ever seen slid to a stop beside them. The living locomotive pawed the ground and snorted. "This is *my* meadow now!" the bull roared.

The rabbit and the cat scampered away in opposite directions. It was clear that from now on, the meadow would not welcome either of them.

1. *Crept like a shadow* is one example of a simile in this passage. What is another?

   _____

2. *The sea of tall grass* is one example of a metaphor in this passage. What is another?

   _____

3. The animals' ability to talk is an example of personification. What is another example from the passage?

   _____

2. Choose two of the literary devises from the passage. Explain the meaning of each.

   _____

   _____

   _____

School–Home Connection

Work with your child to identify examples
of figurative language in a favorite story.
Encourage your child to tell what kind of
figurative language each example represents.

Name _____

▶ Fold the paper along the dotted line. As each Spelling Word
is read aloud, write it in the blank. Then unfold your paper
and check your work. Practice writing any Spelling Words
you missed.

1. _____

2. _____

3. _____

4. _____

5. _____

6. _____

7. _____

8. _____

9. _____

10. _____

11. _____

12. _____

13. _____

14. _____

15. _____

16. _____

17. _____

18. _____

19. _____

20. _____

Spelling Words

1. addresses
2. armies
3. calves
4. countries
5. leaves
6. buses
7. videos
8. echoes
9. shelves
10. studios
11. radios
12. halves
13. hooves
14. knives
15. taxes
16. tomatoes
17. opportunities
18. volcanoes
19. stitches
20. wolves

School–Home Connection

Have your child write ten sentences using all
the Spelling Words. Ask your child to circle the
plural ending in each Spelling Word.

143

Name _____

▶ **Underline the verb phrase in each sentence. Then identify the tense of each one as *present perfect, past perfect,* or *future perfect.***

1. The class has gone on a field trip to the science museum. _____

2. When they return, they will have learned about city habitats.

   _____

3. Jenny had decided to write her science paper on birds that live in cities.

   _____

4. The library will have closed long before she arrives.

   _____

5. Who has borrowed my science book? _____

6. Yvonne had said Jenny could use her book. _____

▶ **Write a sentence using each verb. Use the verb tense shown in parentheses ( ).**

7. draw (present perfect)

   _____

8. choose (past perfect)

   _____

9. paint (future perfect)

   _____

10. help (present perfect)

    _____

11. make (past perfect)

    _____

12. improve (present perfect)

    _____

School–Home Connection

Ask your child to write a list of three verbs.
Then ask him or her to write the present-
perfect, past-perfect, and future-perfect form
of each one.

Practice Book
© Harcourt • Grade 5

► **Which example is better? Underline the phrase or sentence.**

Word	Example 1	Example 2
1. loathe	"I hate that!"	"I love that!"
2. bland	a hot tamale	a bowl of rice
3. mentor	a breath mint	a role model
4. dilapidated	a building missing its windows or doors	a new airplane
5. coordination	a missed train	a perfect football play
6. altruism	work that benefits others	work that benefits yourself
7. sensibility	an allergic reaction	a natural talent or ability for something
8. advocacy	standing up for the rights of others	making sure you get your way
9. mistreated	"Here, have an apple."	"No food or water for you!"
10. compassionate	"I'm sorry you are feeling bad. Can I help?"	"Too bad, you lose."

School–Home Connection

Ask your child to explain to you the meaning of each Vocabulary Word. Then take turns using the words in sentences that show their meaning.

145

Name _____

▶ Read the passage. Then think about the author's purpose
and perspective. Use your ideas and evidence from the
passage to fill in the graphic organizer.

As soon as the postal carrier left, Zeke grabbed the package and tore off the brown paper wrapping. "It's here!" he yelled. "My bat box is here!" Zeke gleefully held up a wooden box that looked like a cross between a birdhouse and a mailbox.

"We keep *our* bats in the closet," said Martin, "with the balls and mitts." He glanced at the wooden box and added, "I think you got the wrong size."

"It's not for that kind of bat," Zeke replied. "This is a house for *live* bats. If I'm lucky, bats will see the house and make a nest inside it. Pretty soon I'll have my own personal bat colony."

Martin shivered and made a face. "Creepy!" he said. "Why would you want to attract a bunch of flying reptiles?"

"They're flying *mammals*," Zeke said. "And it's not creepy—it's smart. Did you know that bats eat thousands of mosquitoes and other pests every night? They help pollinate flowers, and they can distribute the seeds they eat. Plus, they are gentle and totally fun to watch." Zeke lifted the lid of his bat box and peered inside. "Perfect for a big bat family!" he said.

Evidence	Evidence	Evidence

Author's Purpose:

Author's Perspective:

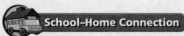
School–Home Connection
Read a magazine with your child, and discuss
the author's purpose and perspective.

146

Practice Book
© Harcourt • Grade 5

Name _____

▶ **Read the passage. Then follow the instructions below the passage.**

> Carlos wiped away another tear and kept chopping. He was halfway through his second onion, and he had three more onions to chop. "I can't believe how much these onions sting my eyes!" he complained.
>
> Medina, the head chef, was busy dropping chunks of spicy ground beef into a big red frying pan. Each chunk sizzled as it landed, filling the air with a rich aroma. "I know," she said with compassion. "Unfortunately, that is the price we pay for good spaghetti sauce."
>
> Carlos sighed and reached for onion number three. He loved the rich, tangy flavor of homemade spaghetti sauce. He also knew that the crowd of volunteers would be as hungry as locusts after their day of beach cleaning. They would definitely appreciate his and Medina's efforts.

▶ **Write *touch*, *sight*, *taste*, *smell*, or *hearing* next to each example of imagery from the passage.**

Example of Imagery	Sense It Appeals To
big red frying pan	
each chunk sizzled	
these onions sting my eyes	
filling the air with a rich aroma	
the rich, tangy flavor of homemade spaghetti sauce	

▶ **Write an answer to each question.**

- Where are Carlos and Medina? How do you know? _____

_____

- How hungry will their guests be? How do you know? _____

_____

_____

School–Home Connection

Ask your child to describe his or her favorite food, using details that appeal to the five senses.

147

Practice Book
© Harcourt • Grade 5

▶ **Read the stories below. Then answer the questions.**

Rattlesnake Tells the Truth, a Native American folktale

One day a man found an injured rattlesnake lying on a rock. The poor snake was nearly dead. The man took pity on the creature and brought it home. Every day he fed it, and little by little the snake regained its health. One morning the man opened the snake's cage to feed it, and the snake bit his hand. Shocked, the man leaped back and gasped, "Why did you do that? I saved your life!"

The creature replied, "Foolish human. I am a snake, and that is what snakes do."
MESSAGE: Everything acts according to its nature.

The Dog and His Reflection, a fable from Greece

A dog was lucky enough to find a large piece of meat. Pleased with himself, the dog picked up the meat in his mouth and started trotting toward home. On the way, the dog crossed a bridge over a small stream. He looked down and was surprised to see another dog with an even bigger piece of meat in its mouth. The dog on the bridge was determined to take the larger piece for himself. When he opened his mouth to snatch the meat, his own piece of meat fell into the stream and sank out of sight.
MESSAGE: If you are too greedy, you may lose everything.

---

1. How are the two stories alike?_____

_____

_____

2. How are the two stories different? _____

_____

_____

_____

School–Home Connection

Share with your child traditional stories from your own culture or stories you know from other cultures. Together, discuss the characteristics of each story.

148

Name _____

> **Read the passage. Then complete the chart.**

As Samantha named off each item on their list, James confirmed the information and checked it off the list. "Fifty garbage bags . . . check! Twenty-five pairs of rubber gloves . . . check! Recycling bins . . . ten for glass and ten for metal . . . check!"

Samantha asked, "Did you remember to call the recycling center and make sure that it will be open?" James nodded. "How about Mr. Larson and his big truck? Did you arrange for him to bring it when we finish?" James nodded again.

Within 15 minutes they were all done with the inventory. Samantha declared that they were ready to start loading supplies into the car.

Textual Evidence	Prior Knowledge	Conclusions

School–Home Connection

Read a story with your child. Use a Draw Conclusions chart like the one on this page to help your child draw conclusions about story events.

149

Name _____

▶ Fold the paper along the dotted line. As each Spelling Word
is read aloud, write it in the blank. Then unfold your paper
and check your work. Practice writing any Spelling Words you
missed.

1. _____

2. _____

3. _____

4. _____

5. _____

6. _____

7. _____

8. _____

9. _____

10. _____

11. _____

12. _____

13. _____

14. _____

15. _____

16. _____

17. _____

18. _____

19. _____

20. _____

Spelling Words

1. indecisive
2. outpatient
3. downgrade
4. uptight
5. acceleration
6. demolition
7. pension
8. champion
9. authorization
10. cancellation
11. autumn
12. knowledge
13. rhyme
14. scenery
15. wrestled
16. armies
17. shelves
18. radios
19. tomatoes
20. videos

Practice Book
© Harcourt • Grade 5

Read this part of a student's rough draft. Then answer the questions below.

(1) It is the day of the big charity soccer match, and Jenna feel nervous. (2) She _____ on her bed and pulls on her new soccer shoes. (3) Jenna's mom is excited as she starts the car and drives Jenna to the match. (4) Jenna play her best soccer ever during today's match! (5) All of her friends cheers her on. (6) After the match, she _____ the trophy high above her head!

1. Which sentence has an action verb that does NOT agree with its singular subject?
   - A Sentence 1
   - B Sentence 3
   - C Sentence 4
   - D Sentence 5

2. Which is a linking verb in Sentence 3?
   - A is
   - B as
   - C starts
   - D drives

3. Which verb could complete Sentence 2?
   - A sets
   - B set
   - C sits
   - D sit

4. Which sentence has an action verb that does NOT agree with its plural subject?
   - A Sentence 1
   - B Sentence 3
   - C Sentence 4
   - D Sentence 5

5. Which verb could complete Sentence 6?
   - A raises
   - B raise
   - C rises
   - D rise

6. Which sentence has a linking verb that does NOT agree with its subject?
   - A Sentence 1
   - B Sentence 3
   - C Sentence 4
   - D Sentence 5

▶ **Read this part of a student's rough draft. Then answer the questions below.**

> (1) Ms. Luiz will have given the order to start digging. (2) She had asked everyone to join in the hard work. (3) "I told the mayor that we had completed this garden by 5:00 P.M. today!" said Ms. Luiz. (4) "Julio, what had you done with your shovel?" she asked. (5) After many hours, the crew of workers finished all of the planting and watering. (6) By the time she leaves, Ms. Luiz will have thanked every volunteer.

1. Which verb form should replace the underlined words in Sentence 1?
   A have given
   B had given
   C giving
   D give

2. Which form of the verb *ask* is used in Sentence 2?
   A past-perfect tense
   B present-perfect tense
   C present tense
   D future tense

3. In Sentence 3, how could the verb *complete* be changed to future-perfect tense?
   A complete
   B will have completed
   C had completed
   D have completed

4. Which verb form should replace the underlined words in Sentence 4?
   A have done
   B were done
   C are done
   D correct as is

5. Which sentence correctly uses a verb in the past tense?
   A Sentence 1
   B Sentence 3
   C Sentence 5
   D Sentence 6

6. Which is the verb tense of the underlined verb phrase in Sentence 6?
   A present-perfect tense
   B future-perfect tense
   C past-perfect tense
   D future tense

▶ **Use what you know about the Vocabulary Words to answer the following questions.**

1. Is an *asset* something that helps you or something that hurts you?

   _____

2. Which action should be done *intently*, driving a car or humming a tune?

   _____

3. Would you thank someone *profusely* for picking up your pencil or for rescuing your dog?

   _____

4. Which task would be an *ordeal*, folding a napkin or moving a piano?

   _____

5. Which is an example of *terrain*, a rocky mountain trail or a thunderstorm?

   _____

6. Would a *dismal* sight fill you with pleasure or make you feel sad?

   _____

7. Should people avoid *peril*, or should they seek it out?

   _____

8. If you *esteem* something, do you admire it or look down on it?

   _____

School-Home Connection

Work with your child to write a story in which you use at least four Vocabulary Words.

153

Practice Book
© Harcourt • Grade 5

▶ As you read each section of "Lewis and Clark," fill in the sequence chart below.

Section 1	pages 666–667

```
┌─────────────────────────────────────────────┐
│                                             │
│                                             │
│                                             │
└─────────────────────────────────────────────┘
```

Section 2	pages 668–671

⬇

```
┌─────────────────────────────────────────────┐
│                                             │
│                                             │
│                                             │
└─────────────────────────────────────────────┘
```

Section 3	pages 672–673

⬇

```
┌─────────────────────────────────────────────┐
│                                             │
│                                             │
│                                             │
└─────────────────────────────────────────────┘
```

▶ Write a summary of "Lewis and Clark."

```
┌─────────────────────────────────────────────┐
│                                             │
│                                             │
│                                             │
│                                             │
│                                             │
│                                             │
│                                             │
└─────────────────────────────────────────────┘
```

▶ **Read the passage. Then follow the directions.**

Before Meriwether Lewis led the famous Corps of Discovery expedition, he was President Thomas Jefferson's private secretary. Lewis had discussed the idea of an expedition to the Pacific many times with the President. However, the Louisiana Territory belonged to France, and Americans would need the permission of the French government to explore it. The purchase of the Louisiana Territory in 1803 removed this obstacle. The American government was free to explore its newest territory, and Lewis was able to fulfill his dream of discovery.

1. On the lines below, write a summary of the paragraph.

_____

_____

_____

_____

_____

_____

2. Paraphrase the first sentence of the passage above.

_____

_____

_____

_____

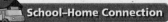
School–Home Connection

Read the paragraph above with your child.
Then take turns restating the sentences in your
own words.

Practice Book
© Harcourt • Grade 5

▶ **Read the passage below. Then answer the questions.**

Lewis and Clark returned to St. Louis with a boatload of treasures. These treasures were not worth a lot of money. They were valuable because of what they contributed to scientific knowledge.

The explorers brought back 39 dried, pressed plants. Nineteen of them were completely new to scientists. They brought back two live animals—a rodent called a prairie dog and a bird called a magpie. They also brought the skins and skeletons of several animals no scientists had ever seen. These included a badger, an antelope, a bighorn sheep, a coyote, and an elk.

The Corps of Discovery brought back valuable knowledge about Native Americans, as well. They recorded the location and number of more than 50 Native American groups.

1. What judgment does the writer make in the first paragraph?

_____

_____

_____

2. Do you think that the plants and animals brought to St. Louis should be considered treasures? Use details from the text to support your answers.

_____

_____

_____

3. Do you think it was right for the explorers to bring back the prairie dog and the magpie? Why or why not?

_____

_____

_____

Practice Book
© Harcourt • Grade 5

Name _____

▶ **Fold the paper along the dotted line. As each Spelling
Word is read aloud, write it in the blank. Then unfold
your paper and check your work. Practice writing any
Spelling Words you missed.**

1. _____

2. _____

3. _____

4. _____

5. _____

6. _____

7. _____

8. _____

9. _____

10. _____

11. _____

12. _____

13. _____

14. _____

15. _____

16. _____

17. _____

18. _____

19. _____

20. _____

Spelling Words

1. unsuccessful
2. undoubtedly
3. impossibly
4. disloyalty
5. deactivation
6. unlikable
7. replacement
8. unsafely
9. uncollectible
10. immeasurable
11. impassible
12. encouragement
13. unbelievable
14. unselfishly
15. rearrangement
16. discoverable
17. dishonestly
18. unbreakable
19. reappearance
20. reassurance

School–Home Connection

Have your child write the Spelling Words
in alphabetical order and then in reverse
alphabetical order.

Practice Book
© Harcourt • Grade 5

Name _____

▶ Complete each sentence with a verb form from the box.
Then label each verb form as *present participle, past tense,* or
past participle.

| blew | rode | saw | were biting | had ridden |

1. When traveling over land, the men _____ on ponies.

   _____

2. Lewis _____ many miles. _____

3. The explorers _____ storm clouds gathering.

   _____

4. The wind _____ most of the clouds away.

   _____

5. However, insects _____ them all night.

   _____

▶ Complete each sentence, using the verb and the verb form shown in parentheses ( ).

6. (*rest,* present participle)

   The group _____ after a long day of walking.

7. (*drink,* past participle)

   Someone _____ the last of the water.

8. (*hear,* past)

   The men _____ the sound of running water.

9. (*run,* present participle)

   Someone _____ ahead to find the source.

10. (*come,* past participle)

    At last, they _____ to the Columbia River!

School–Home Connection

Ask your child to make a list of four action
verbs. Have him or her tell you the present
participle, past tense, and past participle of
each verb.

Practice Book
© Harcourt • Grade 5

Name _____

▶ **Write each Vocabulary Word next to its meaning.**

remote	laden	appalled	invest
grueling	isolated	floundered	

1. _____ weighed down

2. _____ far away from cities, roads, and stores

3. _____ spend money with the hope of making money

4. _____ shocked or extremely surprised in a negative way

5. _____ moved or behaved awkwardly

6. _____ exhausting and difficult

7. _____ all by itself

▶ **Use what you know about the Vocabulary Words to answer each question.**

8. If you lived in a very hot place, what might be a good business to **invest** in?

_____

9. If you saw a family **laden** with suitcases, what might you conclude?

_____

School–Home Connection

Work with your child to use each Vocabulary
Word in a sentence.

159

Name _____

▶ As you read each section of "Klondike Kate," fill in the sequence chart below.

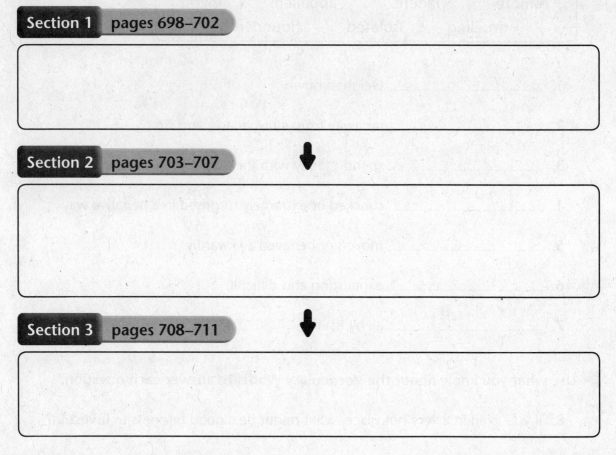

Section 1 pages 698–702

Section 2 pages 703–707

Section 3 pages 708–711

▶ Write a summary of "Klondike Kate."

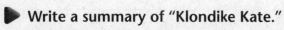

Practice Book
© Harcourt • Grade 5

Name _____

▶ **Read the paragraph below. Then answer the questions.**

> In early 1848, a team of workers led by James Marshall was camped on the
> American River near Sacramento, California. They were building a saw mill for John
> Sutter. On January 24, 1848, Marshall found a few small gold nuggets along the
> river. Just a few months after Marshall's discovery, gold was found in other rivers in
> California. General John Bidwell found gold in the Feather River, and Major Pearson
> Reading discovered gold in the Trinity River. These discoveries led to the California
> gold rush. Approximately 500,000 people traveled to California to seek their fortunes.

1. On the lines below, write a summary of the paragraph.

_____

_____

_____

_____

2. Now paraphrase the first sentence of the passage.

_____

_____

_____

_____

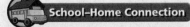

School–Home Connection

Read the paragraph above with your child.
Then take turns restating the sentences in your
own words.

161

Name _____

Fold the paper along the dotted line. As each Spelling Word is read aloud, write it in the blank. Then unfold your paper and check your work. Practice writing any Spelling Words you missed.

1. _____

2. _____

3. _____

4. _____

5. _____

6. _____

7. _____

8. _____

9. _____

10. _____

11. _____

12. _____

13. _____

14. _____

15. _____

16. _____

17. _____

18. _____

19. _____

20. _____

Spelling Words

1. astronomy
2. disaster
3. asterisk
4. astronaut
5. asteroid
6. chronic
7. chronicle
8. chronology
9. chronological
10. synchronize
11. cyclical
12. bicyclist
13. cyclone
14. encyclopedia
15. hydrogen
16. hydrant
17. hydrate
18. optic
19. optician
20. optical

School–Home Connection

Have your child write the Spelling Words on slips of paper. Play Go Fish and try to collect sets of words that share the same root.

Practice Book
© Harcourt • Grade 5

Name _____

▶ Write the contraction for the underlined words in each sentence.

1. She is a daring explorer. _____

2. They are thinking about returning to California. _____

3. They are not finding gold here anymore. _____

4. We are out of food. _____

5. You have got two days to make a decision. _____

6. She could not make up her mind. _____

7. I have not had time to decide. _____

8. "I am too tired to plan anything," said the woman. _____

9. "It is time to stop dreaming and go home," he said. _____

10. It should not take very long to pack. _____

11. You will not have to travel so far this time. _____

12. He has found a new trail. _____

13. They still had not decided on a plan. _____

▶ Underline the word that correctly completes each sentence.

14. (Its, It's) cold and windy today.

15. (Their, They're) leaving in an hour.

16. (Your, You're) horses are prepared for travel.

17. (Their, They're) saddles are clean and ready.

18. (Your, You're) going to be late.

 School–Home Connection

Ask your child to write ten sentences that include contractions. Then ask him or her to rewrite each sentence, replacing each contraction with the words it stands for.

Practice Book
© Harcourt • Grade 5

▶ **Which example is better? Underline the answer.**

Word	Example 1	Example 2
1. summit	Nick added two numbers to find the answer.	Jan climbed to the top of the hill and grinned.
2. accustomed	Laura was used to the summer rainstorms.	Terry had never seen it rain in July.
3. secure	Strong bolts held the hammock in place.	"Whoa!" Martin yelled as he stepped onto the creaky deck.
4. essential	Rhonda took a water bottle on her hike.	Rita put a battery-powered TV in her backpack.
5. streamlined	A bullet train sped through the countryside.	An old car sputtered and lurched down the road.
6. acclimate	Richard observed a monkey in the pet shop window.	Ron learned to live with the constant chatter of chimps.

▶ **Answer the questions below.**

7. How could you help a new student become *accustomed* to your school?

_____

8. Which is *essential* to bring when you travel, a book, a fishing rod, or a toothbrush?

_____

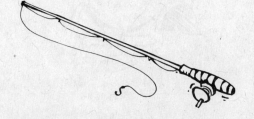

School–Home Connection

Discuss the Vocabulary Words with your child.
Then work together to make up an adventure
story that uses some of the words

Practice Book
© Harcourt • Grade 5

▶ Read each section of "The Top of the World: Climbing Mount Everest." Then fill in the parts of the K-W-L chart.

What I Know	What I Want to Know	What I Learned
		Pages 727–729
		Pages 730–734
		Pages 735–739

▶ On another sheet of paper, write a summary of "The Top of the World: Climbing Mount Everest." Use the facts in the third column to help you.

▶ **Read the passage. Then fill in the chart.**

Mount McKinley is North America's tallest mountain. It is also the hardest mountain in the world to climb. Mount McKinley is part of the Alaska Range. It is located in Denali National Park. The first climber who claimed to reach the summit was Frederick Cook in 1906. Since then, many people of different ages and abilities have climbed Mount McKinley. In 1993, Joan Phelps became the first blind person to climb Mount McKinley. In 1995, Merrick Johnston became the youngest girl to climb the mountain. She was 12-years-old. These are the most amazing ascents by mountain climbers so far.

Statement	Fact or Opinion?	Evidence
Mount McKinley is North America's tallest mountain.		
Mount McKinley is the hardest mountain in the world to climb.		
In 1995, Merrick Johnston became the youngest girl to climb the mountain.		
In 1993, Joan Phelps became the first blind person to climb Mount McKinley.		
These are the most amazing ascents by mountain climbers so far.		

School–Home Connection

Read a magazine article or watch a TV news report with your child. Work together to identify one fact and one opinion.

Practice Book
© Harcourt • Grade 5

Name _____

▶ **Look at the graphs. Then answer the questions below.**

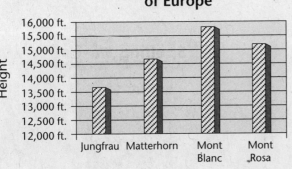

Mountain Peaks of Europe

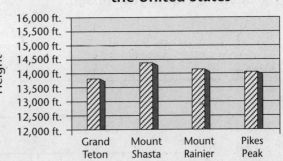

Mountain Peaks of the United States

1. How are the two graphs different?

_____

_____

_____

2. How are the two graphs alike?

_____

_____

3. If you want to climb a European mountain that is between 14,500 and 15,000 feet high, which one would you choose?

_____

4. Do the graphs make information easy to understand? Why or why not?

_____

_____

School–Home Connection

Work with your child to find a graphic source in one of his or her textbooks. Have your child tell you how the graphic source complements the information in the text.

167

Name _____

▶ Fold the paper along the dotted line. As each Spelling
Word is read aloud, write it in the blank. Then unfold
your paper and check your work. Practice writing any
Spelling Words you missed.

1. _____

2. _____

3. _____

4. _____

5. _____

6. _____

7. _____

8. _____

9. _____

10. _____

11. _____

12. _____

13. _____

14. _____

15. _____

16. _____

17. _____

18. _____

19. _____

20. _____

Spelling Words

1. tractor
2. distract
3. traction
4. contract
5. attract
6. subtract
7. erupt
8. bankrupt
9. interrupt
10. abrupt
11. rupture
12. audio
13. audible
14. audience
15. auditorium
16. audition
17. verdict
18. diction
19. dictate
20. predict

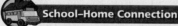

School–Home Connection

Hold a mini Spelling Bee. Call out the words
and have your child spell them aloud. Ask him
or her to write any misspelled words.

168

Name _____

▶ Underline the word or words that correctly complete each sentence.

1. The group sits (quiet, quietly) in the plane.

2. Daeshaun prepares (more eagerly, most eagerly) than Tom.

3. This jump is (easy, easily) for him.

4. Corrine (slowly, slow) fastens her belt.

5. Hal puts on his parachute (fast, faster) than Sue.

6. He (soon, soonest) gets ready.

7. I fly a plane (well, better) than my sister.

8. Rae skydives (well, better).

▶ If the sentence is correct, write *correct*. If it is incorrect, rewrite it correctly.

9. I don't know nothing about trapeze artists.

_____

10. He hasn't never seen the circus.

_____

11. Marcy does not have no time to learn the routine.

_____

12. She has not had none all week.

_____

13. I would do anything to fly high like that!

_____

14. They don't never manage to finish the show on time.

_____

School–Home Connection

Ask your child to write a list of adverbs. Then ask him or her to write sentences, using those adverbs to compare actions.

Practice Book
© Harcourt • Grade 5

Name _____

▶ **Use what you know about the Vocabulary Words to answer
the following questions.**

1. Would it be safe to hold an *ignited* piece of paper? Explain.

    _____

    _____

2. What could *potentially* ruin an outdoor volleyball game?

    _____

    _____

3. Why would it be hard to travel in a *cramped* car?

    _____

    _____

4. What kind of objects might the crew of a sinking ship have *jettisoned*?

    _____

    _____

5. Describe what a person's eyes look like when he is *squinting*.

    _____

    _____

6. How might a person feel if she was in a place of *tranquility*?

    _____

    _____

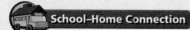

School–Home Connection

Work with your child to write a story using all
the Vocabulary Words.

Practice Book
© Harcourt • Grade 5

Before you read, fill in the first two columns of the chart. Then, as you read each section of "The Man Who Went to the Far Side of the Moon," fill in the third column to show what you learned.

What I **K**now	What I **W**ant to Learn	What I **L**earned
		Astronaut (pages 754–755)
		Blast Off! (pages 756–757)
		Round-Trip to the Moon (pages 758–761)
		On the Moon (pages 762–765)

Name _____

▶ **Read the following paragraph. Then fill in the chart.**

> Black holes are one of the greatest mysteries of our time. A conversation about black holes will always engage both scientists and students. Scientists say that a black hole is a part of space which has such a powerful gravitational force that nothing can escape from it—not even light. There are probably millions of black holes in our galaxy. So far, no one has positively identified a black hole. Astronomers did make an intriguing discovery in 1994, though. Using the Hubble Space Telescope, they found evidence that a black hole exists at the center of M87, another galaxy.

Statement	Fact or Opinion?	Clue Words and Evidence
Black holes are one of the greatest mysteries of our time.		
A conversation about black holes will always engage both scientists and students.		
A black hole is a part of space which has such a powerful gravitational force that nothing can escape from it—not even light.		
Using the Hubble Space Telescope, they found evidence that a black hole exists at the center of M87, another galaxy.		

School–Home Connection

Read a magazine article or listen to a TV news report with your child. Work with him or her to identify facts and opinions in it.

Practice Book
© Harcourt • Grade 5

Name _____

▶ Fold the paper along the dotted line. As each Spelling Word is read aloud, write it in the blank. Then unfold your paper and check your work. Practice writing any Spelling Words you missed.

1. _____

2. _____

3. _____

4. _____

5. _____

6. _____

7. _____

8. _____

9. _____

10. _____

11. _____

12. _____

13. _____

14. _____

15. _____

16. _____

17. _____

18. _____

19. _____

20. _____

Spelling Words

1. banana
2. chimpanzee
3. yogurt
4. almanac
5. syrup
6. cousin
7. stomach
8. language
9. foyer
10. acronym
11. chlorine
12. kayak
13. parka
14. balcony
15. replica
16. anchor
17. urban
18. coyote
19. chocolate
20. vanilla

School–Home Connection

Have your child choose ten Spelling Words to illustrate. Ask them to label each picture with the Spelling Word it shows.

173

▶ **Rewrite the parts of a letter. Use capital letters and correct punctuation.**

1. dear monty _____

2. your friend _____

3. dear sir or madam _____

4. sincerely yours _____

5. write soon _____

6. dear mrs barnes _____

7. yours truly _____

8. 847 north waterview drive _____

9. chicago il 60613 _____

10. april 17, 2008 _____

▶ **Rewrite each sentence. Use correct punctuation. Underline words that should be *italic*.**

11. maybe we can write a report about neil armstrong suggested anne

_____

12. that's a good idea said diane let's get started

_____

13. Mai read the chapter laika to her sister

_____

14. our universe is a popular book

_____

School–Home Connection

Ask your child to write down his or her favorite book title, chapter title, and song title, making sure to use correct punctuation. Your child should underline words that should be *italic*.

174

Name _____

▶ **Which example is better? Underline the word or phrase.**

Word	Example 1	Example 2
1. poised	crouched at the starting line	napping on a couch
2. earnestly	jokingly	truthfully
3. insufficient	too much	not enough
4. exceptional	outstanding movie	dull movie
5. achievement	eating lunch	building a robot
6. bickering	arguing	agreeing
7. equivalent	ten pennies and a dollar	ten pennies and a dime
8. regal	proud poodle	cheese sandwich
9. customary	breakfast at night	breakfast in the morning
10. provoke	tease a zoo animal	watch a zoo animal

Practice Book
© Harcourt • Grade 5

Name _____

▶ **Read the passage. Then follow the directions.**

The manatee is a large, peaceful creature that lives in warm coastal waters from Louisiana to Virginia. Sadly, the manatee is in danger. Manatees like to rest just below the surface of the water. Many manatees have been hit by speeding boaters who do not see them. It is common to find wild manatees with scars on their skin from boating accidents. Places like Florida's Everglades National Park are trying to protect the manatee. In the park, boaters must travel at a very slow speed. Strict boating rules make areas safe for manatees.

1. On the lines below, write a summary of the paragraph.

_____

_____

_____

_____

_____

2. Now paraphrase the last sentence of the passage above.

_____

_____

_____

_____

_____

School–Home Connection

Read the paragraph above with your child.
Then take turns restating the sentences in your
own words.

Practice Book
© Harcourt • Grade 5

▶ **Read the passage. Then fill in the chart.**

The leatherback sea turtle is the fourth-largest reptile in the world. One turtle can weigh as much as 2,000 pounds. Despite their large size, leatherbacks are at risk of injury both in the ocean and on land. Pollution in the ocean, such as oil, rubber, plastic, and tar, endangers the turtles. Also, turtles can get caught in fishing nets. For this reason, fishing boats should not be allowed in the places where turtles swim. Leatherbacks lay their eggs on beaches. Birds, dogs, and human activity can destroy turtle eggs on the beach. We should construct fences on all beaches where leatherbacks lay eggs.

Statement	Fact or Opinion?	Evidence
The leatherback sea turtle is the fourth-largest reptile in the world.		
One turtle can weigh as much as 2,000 pounds.		
Pollution in the ocean, such as oil, rubber, plastic, and tar, endangers the turtles.		
For this reason, fishing boats should not be allowed in the places where turtles swim.		
We should construct fences on all beaches where leatherbacks lay eggs.		

School–Home Connection

Read a magazine article or watch a TV news report with your child. Work together to identify one fact and one opinion.

177

► Read the passage below. Then answer the questions.

The nature magazine David and Melissa worked for had asked them to take photographs of a wild river that runs deep in the rain forest in Nicaragua. The photographers had been hiking for nine hours, and they hadn't found the river.

"Melissa, we need to head back to camp. It will be dark soon," David insisted.

"No way," Melissa shot back. "I'm not leaving until we find the river and take the photographs. This is the most important assignment we've ever had!"

David considered returning to camp without Melissa, but he was scared to be by himself. Returning alone could put Melissa in danger, too.

"Come on," Melissa demanded. "Let's go!" David sighed and continued behind her. They climbed to a top of a small hill and looked down. There was the river.

"See, I told you!" Melissa smiled as she gave him a high five.

1. Why does David want to head back to camp?

_____

_____

2. Do you think it is right that Melissa demanded that David continue with her? Explain.

_____

_____

3. Do you think David should have returned to camp without Melissa? Why or why not?

_____

_____

School–Home Connection

With your child, discuss a character in a movie, a TV show, or a book you are both familiar with. Make a judgment about how that character behaves, how the character spends his or her time, or about another aspect of the character. Use examples to support your judgment.

Practice Book

Name _____

► Look at the graph. Then answer the questions below.

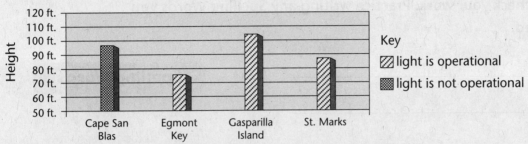

Florida Gulf Lighthouses

Key
⬚ light is operational
▨ light is not operational

1. What information does the graph show? _____

_____

2. How does the key help you read the graph? _____

_____

_____

3. In what order would the lighthouses be listed if they were shown from shortest

to tallest? _____

_____

4. Does the graph make information easy to understand? Why or why not?

_____

_____

_____

School–Home Connection

Look through your child's science textbook to find a graphic source. Discuss with your child how the graphic source adds to the information given in the text.

Practice Book
© Harcourt • Grade 5

▶ Fold the paper along the dotted line. As each Spelling Word is read aloud, write it in the blank. Then unfold your paper and check your work. Practice writing any Spelling Words you missed.

1. _____

2. _____

3. _____

4. _____

5. _____

6. _____

7. _____

8. _____

9. _____

10. _____

11. _____

12. _____

13. _____

14. _____

15. _____

16. _____

17. _____

18. _____

19. _____

20. _____

Spelling Words

1. impossibly
2. deactivation
3. immeasurable
4. unbreakable
5. reappearance
6. asteroid
7. chronology
8. cyclone
9. hydrate
10. optical
11. contract
12. bankrupt
13. audible
14. diction
15. almanac
16. language
17. balcony
18. chlorine
19. cousin
20. urban

▶ Read this part of a student's rough draft. Then answer the questions below.

> (1) My friend Ava has lived on Florida's Gulf Coast for two years.
> (2) _____ really fun to visit her. (3) We are both serious bird-watchers.
> (4) We like to use binoculars to watch the birds fly around and build _____
> nests. (5) The birds haven't never disappointed us. (6) We are thinking about taking
> photographs of them next time!

1. Which names the form of the verb *live* used in Sentence 1?

  A past participle

  B present participle

  C past tense

  D infinitive

2. Which word could complete Sentence 2?

  A It'd

  B It'll

  C It's

  D Its

3. Which contraction could replace the underlined words in Sentence 3?

  A We'll

  B We're

  C We've

  D We'd

4. Which pronoun best completes Sentence 4?

  A their

  B they're

  C it's

  D its

5. How should the underlined words in Sentence 5 be written?

  A haven't ever

  B have not never

  C hadn't never

  D have'nt ever

6. Which names the form of the verb *think* used in Sentence 6?

  A past tense

  B past participle

  C present participle

  D infinitive

▶ **Read this part of a student's rough draft. Then answer the questions below.**

(1) Can Neil be persuaded to help us with the play? asked Marla. (2) "If you ask me," said Keisha, "I think Neil will be the easy convinced of all." (3) "Let's find a way to get more students to join the drama club," said Mandy enthusiastically. (4) "I'll ask Mr. Jennings to speak to the class" suggested Kate. (5) "I don't think the students have read macbeth," said Mr. Jennings. (6) "i think the show will go on!" exclaimed Marla.

1. Where should quotation marks be inserted in Sentence 1?
   A after *play?*
   B before *help* and after *play?*
   C before *Can*
   D before *Can* and after *play?*

2. Which form of the underlined adverb in Sentence 2 should be used?
   A most easily
   B more easily
   C easier
   D easiest

3. Which word in Sentence 3 is described by the adverb *enthusiastically*?
   A find
   B get
   C join
   D said

4. Which is missing from Sentence 4?
   A period
   B quotation marks
   C comma
   D capitalization

5. Which is the correct way to write the underlined title of the play in Sentence 5?
   A "macbeth"
   B "Macbeth"
   C *Macbeth*
   D "*Macbeth*"

6. Which is wrong in Sentence 6?
   A period
   B quotation marks
   C comma
   D capitalization

182

Index

COMPREHENSION

Author's purpose and perspective 125, 131, 146

Cause and effect 75

Compare and contrast 63, 85

Draw conclusions 132, 149

Fact and opinion 166, 172, 177

Make generalizations 64

Make inferences 94, 100, 116

Make judgments 156, 178

Main idea and details 106, 112, 117

Summarize and paraphrase 155, 161, 176

Text structure: cause and effect 81, 86

Text structure: compare and contrast 69

Text structure: sequence 44, 50, 55

GRAMMAR

Adjectives and articles 109, 122

Adverbs 169, 182

Clauses and phrases 52, 60

Complete and simple subjects and predicates 22, 30

Compound subjects and predicates 36, 59

Contractions 163, 181

Interjections 11, 29

Nouns

   Common and proper nouns 66, 90

   Singular and plural nouns 72, 90

   Possessive nouns 78, 91

Prepositional phrases 47, 60

Pronouns

   Pronouns and antecedents 83, 91

   Subjective and objective case pronouns 97, 121

   Possessive and reflexive case pronouns 103, 121

Punctuation 174, 182

Practice Book
© Harcourt • Grade 5

Sentences

   Complex sentences 52, 60

   Declarative and interrogative sentences 6, 29

   Imperative and exclamatory sentences 11, 29

   Simple and compound sentences 41, 59

Subjects and predicates 17, 30

Subject-verb agreement 134, 151

Verbs

   Action and linking 128, 151

   Irregular verbs 158, 181

   Main and helping 114, 122

   Past and future tenses 139, 152

   Perfect tenses 144, 152

   Present tense 134, 151

LITERARY RESPONSE AND ANALYSIS

Character's motives 14, 20, 25

Expository forms 70, 87

Literary devices 137, 142, 147

Literary criticism 34, 56

Literary patterns and symbols 95, 148

Narrative forms 4, 26

Persuasive techniques 126

Plot: conflict and resolution 3, 9, 24

Point of view 107, 119

Theme 33, 39, 54

RESEARCH AND INFORMATION SKILLS

Graphic sources 167, 179

Reference sources 45, 57

SPELLING

Borrowed Words 173, 180

Homophones 113, 120

Unusual Plurals 143, 150

Word Parts *-ation, -ition, -sion, -ion* 133, 150

Word Parts *in-, out-, down-, up-* 127, 150

Practice Book
© Harcourt • Grade 5

Words with

Closed Syllables: Short Vowel Patterns 5, 28

Consonant -le 35, 58

Endings /ən/, /əl/, /ər/ 82, 89

Greek Word Parts 162, 180

Inflections -ed and -ing 21, 28

Latin Word Parts 168, 180

Long Vowels and Vowel Digraphs 10, 28

Prefix + Base Word + Suffix 157, 180

Prefixes im-, in, ir, il 96, 120

Prefixes re-, un-, non- 71, 89

Silent Letters 138, 150

Suffixes -able, -ible, -ment, -less 77, 89

Suffixes -ant, -ent, -eer, -ist, ian 102, 120

Suffixes -ous, -eous, -ious 108, 120

Variant Vowels and Diphthongs 16, 28

VCCCV 51, 58

VCCV: Different Medial Consonants 46, 58

VCCV: Same Medial Consonants 40, 58

VCV Pattern 65, 89

VOCABULARY

Selection vocabulary 1, 7, 12, 18, 23, 31, 37, 42, 48, 53, 61, 67, 73, 79, 84, 92, 98, 104, 110, 115, 123, 129, 135, 140, 145, 153, 159, 164, 170, 175

Synonyms and antonyms 101, 118

Using words in context 15, 27

Using word parts 76, 88

Practice Book
© Harcourt • Grade 5